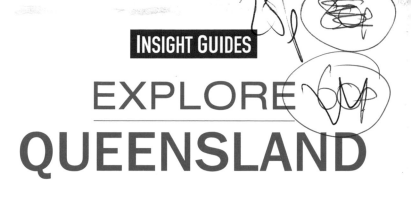

INSIGHT GUIDES

EXPLORE
QUEENSLAND

WITHDRAWN

D0522378

CONTENTS

ADVENTURE-SEEKERS

4WD the world's largest sand islands
– Moreton (route 3), North Stradbroke
(route 5) and Fraser (route 8) – catch
waves on the Sunshine Coast (route 4)
and Gold Coast (route 6), and learn to
scuba-dive.

RECOMMENDED ROUTES FOR...

ANIMAL-LOVERS

Hand-feed a wild dolphin at
Tangalooma (route 3), snorkel amid
kaleidoscopic life on the reef (see
page 26) near Cairns (route 10) and
the Whitsundays (route 9), and meet a
crocodile at Australia Zoo (route 4).

CHILDREN

Whether you're based in Brisbane,
with its urban beach and Big Wheel
(route 2), or the beach mecca of
the Gold Coast (tour 6), it's easy to
access the fun-packed theme parks
(see page 24).

CULTURE

For music, international exhibitions, or
indigenous and modern art, Brisbane
(routes 1 and 2) and Cairns (route 10)
have galleries and art centres that
showcase Queensland's culture.

FOOD AND DRINK

Visit Brisbane's standout bistros (route 1) or Noosa's Hasting Street eateries (route 4) for top-notch food, while Australia's best coffee is grown and brewed on the Atherton Tablelands (route 14).

NATIONAL PARKS

Strap on your walking shoes and hit Queensland's lush national park trails on the Sunshine Coast (route 4), in the Gold Coast hinterland (route 7), Atherton Tablelands (route 14) and en route to Mission Beach (route 15).

NIGHT OWLS

In Brisbane, enjoy a night at the theatre in South Bank's renowned Queensland Performing Arts Complex (route 2) or find a riverside bar (route 1). In Cairns (route 10) visit the casino and the Tanks Art Centre.

ROBINSON CRUSOES

Find peace and solitude on an almost deserted tropical beach in the Whitsunday Islands (route 9). Similar seclusion can be found on the endless empty beaches of North Stradbroke Island (route 5).

INTRODUCTION

An introduction to Queensland's geography, customs and culture, plus illuminating background information on cuisine, history and what to do when you're there.

Brisbane's Story Bridge

EXPLORE QUEENSLAND

From the glittering Gold Coast and bustling capital city of Brisbane to the verdant Wet Tropics, where prehistoric rainforest meets the greatest coral reef on earth, Queensland's amazing coastline is an incredible adventure playground.

Size isn't everything, but it is a factor when considering Queensland. This may be only the second-largest state in Australia (after Western Australia), but its 1.73 million sq km (667,000 sq miles) would comfortably swallow several European countries. However, within this vast area there are only 5 million people – about equivalent to the population of Sydney or Barcelona. In cosmopolitan Brisbane and amid the high-rise high-gratification zone of the Gold Coast it can still seem busy, and people watching is all part of the pull, but travel anywhere else and you'll discover a relaxed, uncrowded and friendly place.

GEOGRAPHY AND LAYOUT

The region covered by the routes featured here is the coast, hinterland and offshore islands between Brisbane and the Gold Coast in the south and Daintree and Cape Tribulation in the north. The routes begin with two walks exploring the historic, entertainment and scenic precincts of the Queensland capital. On Brisbane's doorstep, the natural sand islands of Moreton and North Stradbroke offer scenic 4WD exploration and marine wildlife encounters. Two more easy day trips from Brisbane are provided by the high-rise-backed beaches of the Gold Coast and their counterpoint, the verdant Gold Coast hinterland. The Gold Coast is also the setting for a cluster of theme parks (see page 24).

Heading north, the Sunshine Coast combines an idyllic climate and landscape with gourmet culture, while Fraser Island has a highway of sand for 4WD enthusiasts. In the picturesque Whitsunday Islands, leave your car behind as you island-hop by ferry, camp under the stars and spend your days kayaking and snorkelling.

In Cairns – the capital of far north Queensland and gateway to the Great Barrier Reef – explore the historic town on foot. From Cairns, you can take a ride on a historic train and amazing cable car to and from the market town of Kuranda, or explore the resorts of Port Douglas and Mission Beach, the ancient rainforests of Daintree and Cape Tribulation, and the coffee plantations and waterfalls of the Atherton Tablelands.

Hanggliding off cliffs near Port Douglas

QUEENSLAND'S HISTORY

About 15 million years ago, the Australian continent broke away from an ancient land mass known as Gondwanaland and gradually drifted northwards to its present location. Due to periodic ice ages, sea levels were lower than today; so low that anyone reaching New Guinea from Asia could continue the journey to north Queensland on foot. These first migrants, ancestors of Australia's Aborigines, arrived some 50,000 years ago.

The first Europeans
It is Dutchman Willem Janssen, who sailed into the Gulf of Carpentaria in 1605, who is generally cited as the first European to 'discover' Australia. Another Dutchman, Abel Tasman, charted parts of Tasmania in 1642 and the northern coast from Cape York to Port Hedland two years later. However, credit for charting the eastern coastline goes to Captain James Cook, whose 1770 voyage opened the way to colonisation.

The penal years
In the late 18th century, the east coast of Australia became a dumping ground for Britain's criminals. In 1788 and 1790, fleets of convict ships arrived at Port Jackson, Sydney's great harbour-to-be, and the colony grew. Cook had noted the presence of fresh water in Moreton Bay back in 1770, while in 1799, Lieutenant Matthew Flinders

charted much of the bay but failed to notice the mouth of what is now called the Brisbane River. The river was finally 'discovered' in 1823, when explorer John Oxley was tipped off by some shipwrecked sailors.

An independent Queensland
The first half of the 19th century saw a change in European settlement in Australia. The transportation of convicts was phased out, and by 1860 the continent had been divided into seven col-

Indigenous people

There is no escaping the fact that the indigenous people of Queensland have had a tragic existence since white settlement: killed in huge numbers by imported diseases and settlers' guns, living at the mercy of discriminatory laws and damaged by displacement, alcohol and drugs. There have been decades of government funding and more recently there has been official recognition of the mistakes of the past, but many policies have been misguided or mismanaged.

Among Queensland's many notable Indigenous people are the late poet and activist Kath Walker (whose traditional name is Oodgeroo Noonuccal), William Barton, the Brisbane-based Aboriginal didgeridoo player, the artist Judy Watson, and high-profile achievers such as Olympic gold medallist Cathy Freeman and television personality Ernie Dingo.

Gold Coast high-rises

onies, one of which was Queensland. At that time the European population numbered only 23,520, and no industry had yet been established, although gold had been discovered in 1858.

Federation, war and depression

The Commonwealth of Australia, which included the state of Queensland, was born in 1901 and Brisbane was proclaimed a city the following year. When Britain declared war on Germany in August 1914, Australia, as a member of the British Empire, was automatically at war, too.

In 1923, vast silver-lead-zinc deposits were found inland at Mount Isa, but the Depression of the late 1920s and early 1930s was hard on Queensland. In 1934 the Labor Party stimulated the economy

---

DON'T LEAVE QUEENSLAND WITHOUT...

Meeting a six-foot-tall bird. Your best chance of seeing a cassowary in the wild is around Mission Beach, but don't bank on it – Australia's largest rainforest animal is endangered. You can be certain of seeing one, however, at Cairns Tropical Zoo. See page 80.

Experiencing inland treasures. The coast gets all the press, but be sure to visit the hinterland behind the Gold Coast and Tablelands that overlook Cairns and Port Douglas – these lush hills and plateaus are gorgeous and offer relief from both crowds and oppressive heat. See page 60 and page 88.

Having a close encounter with the Great Barrier Reef. The greatest living organism on the planet is extraordinary up close. Take a snorkel and mask everywhere you go, try an introductory dive, do a day trip or go the whole hog and do a live-aboard dive trip. See page 26.

Riding the ocean waves. Get on a surfboard or paddle across the turquoise waters of the Coral Sea in a kayak or on a SUP board. See page 23.

Loosening your belt. Go on a gastronomic blow out around the fabulous foodie streets of Brisbane – especially James Street, Eagle Street Pier, Little Stanley Street, Merthyr Road in New Farm and Brunswick Street in Fortitude Valley. See page 15.

Going island hopping around the Whitsundays. Seventy-four curvaceous coral cays and tantalising tropical islets lie just begging to be explored by beachcombers, sailors and cast-away types. See page 67.

Earning your off-road wings. Drive a 4WD adventure wagon across the world's biggest sand island, Fraser Island. Watch out for dingoes as you cruise the beach, and keep an eye on the waves for signs of whales. See page 63.

Seeking out an unusual adventure. How about a spot of jungle surfing above the rainforest canopy in the Daintree, or perhaps river snorkelling just outside of Port Douglas? Go with the experts, they know where the crocodiles are... See page 87 and page 83.

Brisbane's General Post Office   *Soaking up the sun on the Sunshine Coast*

through large capital projects, including the construction of Story Bridge and the University of Queensland.

War and boom times

When Britain went to war against Germany in September 1939, Australia once more automatically entered the conflict. Of the 1 million Australian servicemen and women who enlisted, almost 27,000 died.

The 1950s saw the rapid development of the coastal strip south of Brisbane. Originally a secluded holiday destination for Brisbane's middle classes, its property values soared in the post-war period, leading one journalist to dub the area the 'Gold Coast'.

Modern politics: floods and landslides

The long tradition of Queensland being a Labor heartland fell apart in the mid-1950s. After 25 years in power, the party lost the election, ushering in 32 years of rule by the National Party. For two decades until 1987, politics and social life in Queensland were dominated by Sir Joh Bjelke-Petersen, and the era was characterised by confrontation between his government and unions and civil-rights advocates.

When Labor's Peter Beattie – victorious in the 2001 and 2004 elections – retired in 2007, he handed the premiership to Anna Bligh, Queensland's first female premier, who became the first woman to lead her party to a state election victory in 2009.

Between December 2010 and February 2011, large-scale floods devastated Brisbane, killing 35 people and creating a state of emergency. Bligh's handling of the natural disaster was well regarded and she enjoyed a brief period of huge popularity. This was short-lived, however, thanks to vicious infighting within the national Labor party and accusations of the public having been mislead over the sale of assets in Queensland. In the 2012 state election, Labor suffered a major defeat and the Liberal party, led by the former Brisbane Lord Mayor, Campbell Newman, was voted in with the biggest majority in the state's history.

CLIMATE

Queensland has just two seasons: summer (October–March) and winter. The difference is more pronounced in the south. In the north, there is a wet season (mid-December–April), when rainfall and thunderstorms are common. Northern Australia (which includes Tropical Far North Queensland) endures an annual cyclone season, which officially runs from November to April. On 3 February 2011, Severe Tropical Cyclone Yasi ripped through parts of northern Queensland leaving a trail of utter devastation in its wake.

April to September – the Australian autumn and winter – is often the best time to visit Queensland (particularly the north), as rainfall and temperatures are lower.

Performance at the Tjapukai Aboriginal Cultural Park

Brisbane has summer temperatures that range from 20°C to the high 30s (68–86°F plus) and winter temperatures of 10–20°C (35–68°F), with a daily average of eight hours of sunshine. In Cairns the temperature range in winter is 16–26°C (55–90°F) and in summer it can exceed 36°C (125°F), when humidity is also high.

POPULATION AND ECONOMY

According to the 2006 census, about 128,000 Aborigines and Torres Strait Islanders live in Queensland, which is about 3.3 percent of the total population. Queensland has one of the fastest-growing populations of any state in Australia. Part of this increase is from overseas migration; Queensland's primary industries – wheat, fruit, cattle, cotton, sugar cane, viticulture, wool and mining – have depended on the hard work of immigrants from more than 200 nations. Some have congregated, creating atmospheric and vibrant neighbourhoods, such as South Sea Islanders in Mackay and Italians in Innisfail. However, it is the interstate migrants who are changing Queensland most dramatically. They include a lot of prosperous southern baby-boomers and retirees bringing their wealth north to buy property.

The influx has coloured the way the rest of Australia views Queenslanders. Historically, the typical Queenslander was defined by the rugged frontier of the far north and outback, with iconic pioneering status as well as conservative values. Another type resides in the southeast corner, a haven for retirees, where poker machines munch through pensions and high-rises shoot up to go one better than their neighbour.

FUTURE CHALLENGES

There are still thousands of kilometres of Queensland coast where anyone can find their own little piece of paradise. Coastal Queensland has boomed on the back of tourism that understandably relies heavily on the state's natural wonders, particularly the Great Barrier Reef, but there are real threats to this idyllic image. Global warming has been implicated in recent coral-bleaching events, mining and agriculture add to harmful sediment flows and, in 2010, a wayward Chinese coal-carrying vessel, the *Shen Neng*, slammed into the Great Barrier Reef, tearing a 1km-long gash into the reef and spewing oil into the Coral Sea, creating a major environmental disaster and highlighting the growing challenges of conserving the beauty in a rapidly developing Queensland. Despite this warning sign, in December 2013 the Australian government gave the go ahead for further mining activity in the region that will see Queensland's Abbot Point coal port dredged to allow access for bigger and increasing numbers of tankers, with the resulting silt to be dumped within the World Heritage-listed area of the Great Barrier Reef. The decision created wide-

Bungy-jumping near Cairns

The Glasshouse Mountains near the Sunshine Coast

spread horror and condemnation from conservation groups, environmental agencies and the general public within Australia and abroad, and there is a real possibility that UNESCO will now label the Great Barrier Reef as endangered.

TOP TIPS FOR EXPLORING QUEENSLAND

Sun sense. It's not called the Sunshine State for nothing. Queenslanders have the world's highest rate of skin cancer, but they are learning. Make like a local and slip, slop, slap with the sun block (factor 30) and wear hats, sunglasses and – when in the water – rash vests ('rashies').

Get what you pay for. In resorts on the islands, being part of a captive audience can mean paying more for food and drinks. However, if you're not happy with the service you receive in return, tell management about it straight away and give them a chance to make it up to you. Their reputation as a destination depends on happy travellers.

Go bush. Almost all of Queensland's 5-million strong population live around Brisbane or on the coastal strip north to Port Douglas. Tourists mirror this trend, but check out the hinterland and outback areas, where you'll find the most interesting and eccentric people and pubs.

Brisbane on the cheap. Save yourself serious dollars by picking up a Brisbane Five in One card (www.brisbanefiveinone.com), which gets you into a range of attractions including Lone Pine Koala Sanctuary, Story Bridge Adventure Climb, Riverlife Adventure Centre, XXXX Brewery Tour and Kookaburra River Cruises.

Be active. Explore as many places as possible on foot, by bike or with a paddle in your hands. Queensland's weather is there to be enjoyed, plenty of places hire bikes, boats and boards, and if you're going to take full advantage of all the great food here, you'll need to burn off those calories somehow.

BYO fun. Take your own snorkelling gear, or buy a good mask, snorkel and set of fins as soon as you arrive. Incredible snorkelling opportunities are found around every coastal corner in Queensland and some places (island resorts in particular) charge a huge amount for hourly or daily hire.

Theme park packages. The Gold Coast's major theme parks offer various joint packages that provide discounted entry to two or more parks – shop around to get the best deal.

Be warned. Between the end of November and the middle of December, the Gold Coast, particularly Surfers Paradise, is hit by 'Schoolies' – thousands of final-year students on a ritualistic post-exam drunken bender.

Don't become dinner. Saltwater crocodiles live in tidal reaches of rivers, as well as freshwater sections of lagoons, swamps and waterways, and along some beaches and offshore islands. They really are there, and they really might eat you. Always heed warning signs!

Aboriginal bush bread baked over an open fire

FOOD AND DRINK

Queensland's gastronomic credentials are born of two factors: a cultural diversity attracting chefs experienced in some of the world's top cuisines, plus the rich variety of the local produce from tropical seas, rolling pastures and volcanic soils.

Australian cuisine has evolved during 200 years of immigration from almost every country in the world, and the resulting blend of tastes has enriched its dining tables with a huge diversity of cross-cultural concepts. Although British immigrants were in the majority in the early days, Australia's menus were much enhanced by major waves of immigration from China, Italy, Greece and, more recently, Southeast Asia, the Middle East and Africa. In deference to the generally warm subtropical climate, there is now a definite avoidance of some of the heavy, stodgy menus of northern Europe.

The resultant fusion of disparate influences, which tends to disrespect culinary borders, is usually termed modern Australian or 'Mod Oz'. Thus, for example, Asian greens may accompany a Spanish-style seafood dish, the chef relying on the compatibility of the flavours and fresh local ingredients rather than traditional cuisine.

LOCAL CUISINE

The original local cuisine is, of course, 'bush tucker': seasonally available native plants and animals cooked over a campfire. The easiest way to sample these flavours in an authentic way is to join an Aboriginal-guided tour or attend an indigenous venue where bush tucker is on the menu. Alternatively, many of Queensland's more experimental chefs are infusing their dishes with native herbs and spices, while kangaroo, emu and crocodile are now commonly found on menus.

A few decades ago, meat and three veg would have summed up a typical Queensland dinner, and a steak was a steak and the bigger the better. Not any more. Now you must decide between 400-day-old, grass-fed Angus from King Island or 300-day-old Wagyu with 160 days of grain feeding to promote the marbling of the fat. Then there is the decision of which cut to choose and whether to cook it blue, rare or medium. (A quality steak restaurant will never offer to cook a steak 'well done'.)

When it comes to seafood, few places on earth can compete with Queensland. Whatever your taste – be it molluscan, crustacean or piscatorial – Queensland has ample varieties and copious quantities sourced from clean waters. When in Brisbane, ask for More-

Australian barramundi

ton Bay bugs: delicious slipper lobsters with excellent sweet white flesh, perfect for Mediterranean and Asian cooking styles. Up north, two species of fish – barramundi and coral trout – vie for top spot in a long list of delicious contenders. Barramundi ('barra') is an estuarine perch that grows to legendary size and is excellent when cooked bush-tucker-style on hot coals, or sizzled on a BBQ plate, or even from a chip shop. Coral trout is a beautiful, spotted tropical reef fish that perfectly suits Asian cuisine.

WHERE TO EAT

Brisbane claims the highest number of restaurants per capita of any city in Australia, and several neighbourhoods and streets have evolved a popular restaurant scene. The cafés and bistros of Eagle Street Pier (www.eaglestreetpier.com.au), James Street (www.jamesst.com.au/food-drink), Park Road in Milton, Brunswick Street in Fortitude Valley, Merthyr Road in New Farm and Little Stanley Street on South Bank, offer good fare in often sophisticated settings. Most Brisbane precincts have a growing selection of ethnic restaurants, the most common being Thai, Indian and Vietnamese. Asian restaurants are mainly concentrated in Fortitude Valley, West End and Sunnybank.

The Gold Coast has more than 5,000 restaurants, ranging from super-casual surf club bistros, such as Northcliffe Surf Club Bistro, to opulent highrise dining rooms. Noosa has a reputation for quality dining in modish restaurants usually found on or near sophisticated Hastings Street, Noosa Heads.

High-end restaurants

Fine dining is almost exclusively found in the larger commercial centres and upmarket resorts – the sorts of places where you will also find five-star hotels, such as Brisbane, the Gold Coast, Noosa and Cairns, along with the resort islands. And you do not have to look far past the dining rooms of the five-stars to find award-winning chefs performing culinary art for the grateful, and well-heeled, clientele. Brisbane's Cha Cha Char Wine Bar & Grill continues to raise the bar with award-winning steaks, and the Gold Coast's Absynthe delights gourmands with Gallic ingenuity.

Ethnic restaurants

The explosion in inexpensive ethnic cuisine in Australia shows no sign of stopping. Indian, Thai, Turkish, Mexican, Lebanese and Vietnamese have joined the old guard of Italian, Greek and Chinese to rescue folks from resorting to fast food or DIY home cooking, and these are the venues that keep Australia on the cutting edge of the world's cuisine scene. Keep an eye out for the imminent arrival of hipster Asian cuisine (think Peking duck burgers) and even the appearance of a few insects on menus, a la Chinese influence snacks like stir-fried crickets in black-

Kangaroo pie in Kuranda

bean and chilli. Inland the choice may be limited to traditional Chinese and pizza, but coastal Queensland, with its cosmopolitan population and massive tourist market, offers a staggering array of ethnic cuisine. Many restaurateurs maximise the cultural experience with careful attention to detail, such as the Ottoman-tent ambience at Ahmets in Brisbane's South Bank.

Pubs and bistros

Again, it is the demands of inbound and international tourism that has boosted coastal Queensland's pubs from mere fuel stops to purveyors of quality food. Along the backpacker trail are barn-sized pubs selling DIY steaks for punters to cook on communal BBQs or hot volcanic rocks – a fun trend whereby the expertise in timing is left to you rather than a professional cook (no room for complaining). Elsewhere, you will find many a gracious old pub that has been gentrified into a restaurant with an attached bar, rather than the other way round, such as the Straddie Pub and Port Douglas' s Court House Hotel.

DRINKS

Coffee

Queensland's café scene has exploded over the last few years. Great coffee is grown on the Atherton Tablelands near Cairns, and there are plenty of cafés around that support the local growers and roasters. Expert local coffee roasters including Merlo and Di Bella have helped fuel the boom, as has a move towards alfresco eating, and with the rise of a multitude of hipster-pleasing craft coffee joints around Brisbane, if you shut your eyes (and perhaps get in a cold shower) you could be forgiven for thinking that you're in Melbourne. Sample some seriously good bean juice in Brisbane venues such as Brew, Lady Marmalade and Our Haus.

Non-alcoholic drinks

Unsurprisingly, given the tropical climate and the fantastic variety of fruit grown throughout the sunny state, fresh juice bars have become very popular all over Queensland and these are ideal places to get a vitamin and natural sugar fix while attempting to beat the heat.

Wine

The reputation of Australian wines has now fully matured and the country has in excess of 2,500 wineries, many offering cellar-door sales. While the biggest 20 companies produce over 95 percent of Australia's total output, 'boutique wineries' make up well over two-thirds of the total number of wineries. Most people think of the southern states when it come to wine (oak-driven reds and whites from the Barossa Valley in South Australia and the Margaret River region of Western Australia, Chardonnay and aged Semil-

Boutique beers

Bush tucket features fruits of the rainforest

lons from The Hunter Valley in New South Wales, Cabernet Sauvignon from Coonawarra in the southeast of South Australia, Shiraz from Heathcote in Victoria and Pinot Noir from Tasmania), but Queensland does have an emerging wine industry (www.queensland-wine.com.au). Fabulous fruit wines are produced in the far north, while some award-winning reds and whites have emerged from southeast Queensland, especially in the area called the Granite Belt. Local wines are often light, crisp and fruity, and are designed to complement Queensland's food.

If you're spooked by licensed-restaurant wine prices, it is usually not too hard to find an unlicensed BYO (bring your own wine) restaurant. These restaurants normally charge corkage (per person or per bottle), but it's still much cheaper than buying massively marked-up wine – and there is often a strategically placed liquor outlet nearby.

Beer

Australian beers are famous internationally, and are consumed in vast quantities by their domestic devotees. The most popular brew in Queensland is the local XXXX Bitter (Four X). Queensland's detractors claim that it's called this because few Queenslanders could spell 'beer'. Thankfully, increasing varieties of beer are also becoming available, and brewpubs are flourishing as palates become more adventurous and drinkers less con-

servative. Boutique breweries have been popping up everywhere from the backstreets of Brisbane to the beach blocks of Burleigh Heads on the Gold Coast, where the excellent Burleigh Brewing Company creates craft beers with names such as Fanny Gertrude's, Black Giraffe and My Wife's Bitter.

Order your Queensland beer in a 'pot' (a 285ml/10oz glass called a 'middy' in NSW or a 'ten' up north) or a schooner (425ml/15oz). In British- or Irish-themed pubs, pints and half-pints normally rule.

Bush tucker

Early European pioneers learnt a lot about 'bush tucker' and bush medicine from the indigenous population, but their less adventurous countrymen who followed dismissed thousands of years of local knowledge and forced European plants and animals on the land. Two centuries later, many lessons have been learnt, but droughts, weeds and erosion warn that Australians are still learning. Queensland's most celebrated bush food is the macadamia nut, also known as the Queensland nut, which was taken to Hawaii where it became a worldwide commercial success. You will not find many menus dominated by bush foods; however, you will find native fruits, vegetables, herbs and spices flavouring many dishes in fine-dining restaurants. In Cairns, try Ochre Restaurant European flair utilising indigenous ingredients.

Didgeridoo store at a Kuranda market

SHOPPING

With so much to see and do in Queensland's great outdoors you may be forgiven for leaving the shopping until the last minute. But the state's department stores, shopping strips, galleries and markets are well worth exploring.

Throughout Queensland there are ample opportunities to shop for everything from boulder opals to raw cane sugar, didgeridoos to surf gear. Some notable Australian manufacturers have outlets in key shopping and tourism centres – among them is **Akubra**, whose famous broad-brimmed felt hats have become iconic. To complete the look, check out stockists of **RM Williams**, the brand named after the late and legendary bushman who designed and sold practical bush-wear to rural Queenslanders for many years. Queensland-produced foodstuffs are now also very popular, including macadamia nuts in various guises, tea and coffee from plantations in Tropical North Queensland, koala-shaped pasta and, for adventurous carnivores, crocodile, shark or emu jerky.

Most shops are open Mon–Fri 9am–5pm, with extended evening hours to 9pm on either or both Thursday and Friday. Saturday trading is usually 10am–5pm, while larger stores in big centres or tourist precincts will also trade on Sunday 10am–5pm. The major annual sales are after Christmas (from Boxing Day onwards) and at Easter and mid-year, in the lead-up to the end of the Australian financial year (30 June).

BRISBANE

Brisbane's **Queen Street Mall**, the centre of the city's shopping scene, offers more than 700 speciality shops spread across two city blocks, which are dominated by two large department stores, **Myers** and **David Jones**, which sell pretty much everything. The attractive, heritage-listed **Brisbane Arcade** nearby showcases the work of Queensland's award-winning fashion designers.

Fortitude Valley also has a number of retail attractions including the TCB Arcade and Licorice Lane. Gail Sorronda is just one of the designer boutiques on nearby James Street, while the ultra-chic fashion studio Subfusco is located on Gray Road in the city's West End.

Some Aboriginal art is unique, and some is mass-produced. For the former try **Aboriginal Fine Art**, on Albert Street Mall (www.aboriginal-fineart.com; Sat-Thur 10am till 6pm, Fri until 8pm).

South Bank comes alive with stalls at the weekend for the **Collective Markets** (www.collectivemarkets.com.au;

Sculptures by a local artist at Eumundi Markets

Sat 10am–9pm, Sun 9am–4pm), and on a Sunday, check out the **Riverside Craft Market** (8am–4pm) at Eagle Street Pier.

GOLD COAST

The Gold Coast features a number of huge shopping complexes, primary among them the **Centro Surfers Paradise** in Cavill Avenue. Other major malls are **The Oasis** shopping centre, Victoria Avenue, Broadbeach, adjoining Conrad Jupiter's Casino; and **Pacific Fair**, Hooker Boulevard, Broadbeach.

The most reputable market on the Gold Coast is **Carrara Markets** (Sat–Sun 7am–4pm), which is located on the Nerang–Broadbeach Road near Pacific Fair. Aboriginal artefacts are also sold at the new **Jellurgal Aboriginal Cultural Centre** (1711 Gold Coast Highway, Burleigh; www.jellurgal.com.au; Mon Friday 8am-3pm, Saturday to 2pm).

CAIRNS

The main shopping area in Cairns is the Central Business District, roughly bounded by the Esplanade, Shields, Spence and Grafton streets. The **Esplanade Markets** operate every Saturday (8am–4pm) at Fogarty Park and along the Esplanade. Further out of town, the **Tjapukai Aboriginal Gallery** (Kamerunga Road, Caravonica; www.tjapukai.com.au), adjacent to the Kuranda Skyrail terminal, is a showplace of authentic Aboriginal art and artefacts. **Kuranda 'Original' Markets** (5 Therwine Street; www.kurandaoriginalrainforestmarket.com.au; Wed–Fri, Sun 9am–4pm) make for a great shopping excursion from Cairns.

SUNSHINE COAST

All the produce sold at the thriving **Noosa Farmers' Market** (Weyba Road, Noosaville; noosafarmersmarket.com.au; Sun 7am–noon) is produced by the stallholders. About 15 minutes from Noosa, pretty **Eumundi** village draws throngs of tourists and locals to its twice-weekly markets (Wed 8am–1.30pm, Sat 6.30–2pm).

Aboriginal art

A piece of Aboriginal art is one of the most emblematic and evocative souvenirs of a visit to Australia. Aboriginal artists sell their work in community art centres, specialist galleries and through agents. Each artist owns the rights to his or her particular stories, motifs and tokens. Dot and bark paintings are the most common forms of Aboriginal art, but look out for contemporary works on canvas, board, boomerangs and didgeridoos, the Aboriginal musical instrument produced in northern Australia from tree branches hollowed out by termites. Boomerangs are always popular; genuine returning and hunting models usually come with instructions to help you throw them properly (and safely).

Bolshoi Ballet dancers at Queensland Performing Arts Centre

ENTERTAINMENT

Queensland's entertainment scene has blossomed visibly over recent years, and concerts, festivals and celebrations now punctuate the events calendar in Brisbane and the Gold Coast, as well as in far North Queensland.

Thanks to Queensland's sunny outdoor lifestyle and the popularity of team pursuits, the arts usually play second fiddle to sport. Nonetheless, the state has a lot to offer, in part due to the changes brought about by World Expo '88 and the development of the Queensland Cultural Precinct in Brisbane's South Bank, where the Queensland Performing Arts Complex (QPAC; www.qpac.com.au) regularly hosts performers of international renown. Brisbane also nurtures alternative venues devoted to cutting-edge performances and exhibitions. And with more than 35 percent of the state's population living in regional remote centres, touring has become an essential aspect of taxpayer-funded arts organisations. For more on nightlife, see page 120.

THEATRE

Queensland's acting luminaries include Geoffrey Rush, Diane Cilento, Billie Brown and Deborah Mailman, but new talent spotters should check out Brisbane's stylishly grungy Powerhouse (119 Lamington Street, New Farm; brisbanepowerhouse.org), where primarily avant-garde performances are staged among graffiti and industrial machinery, and the lively Judith Wright Centre of Contemporary Arts (420 Brunswick Street, Fortitude Valley; judithwrightcentre.com). The delightfully old-fashioned Brisbane Arts Theatre (210 Petrie Terrace; www.arts-theatre.com.au) continues to produce drawing-room comedies, mysteries and pantomimes as it has since 1936.

MUSIC AND DANCE

The Sunshine State has produced musical talent across a range of genres; local performers and bands include Savage Garden, Powderfinger, george, Pete Murray, Kate Miller-Heidke, Keith Urban, The Veronicas, The Go Betweens, Tex Perkins and The Saints.

The live music scene in Queensland has continued to evolve over the last few years, with new and improved smaller venues leading the charge. Keep an eye on who is appearing on the bill at intimate places such as The Beetle Bar (beetlebar.com.au; 350 Upper Roma St, City) and the Black Bear Lodge (blackbearlodge.com.au; 1/322 Brunswick St, Fortitude Valley). In Cairns, the Tanks Art Centre (www.tanksartcentre.com;

Circus performers at the Woodford Folk Festival

46 Collins Avenue, Edge Hill), out by the Botanic Gardens, is an innovative venue featuring assorted forward-looking musical acts. Brisbane also has a thriving jazz scene, partly centred on the Brisbane Jazz Club at Kangaroo Point, partly in Fortitude Valley bars such as Ric's Bar, The Press Club and The Bowery.

The Queensland Orchestra (www.thequeenslandorchestra.com.au) delivers a programme of more than 70 concerts annually, while the Queensland Ballet Company (www.queenslandballet.com.au) perform mostly at QPAC's Playhouse, with three annual Vis-à-Vis performances at the company's heritage-listed headquarters (424 Montague Road, West End; tel: 3013 6666) – a must if you are keen on dance.

NIGHTLIFE

The heart of Brisbane's nightlife is Fortitude Valley, aka 'The Valley', which has one of Australia's best live music scenes. For up-to-date gig guides, consult the *Courier Mail*, free streetpress publications such as *Scene* magazine, and the listings website: www.brisbane247.com.

Around the Caxton Street/Petrie Terrace intersection are several good venues. Leading the pack are: the **Casablanca** (www.casablanca.com.au), a bar, café and steamy cellar club; the **Hotel LA** (www.hotella.com.au), a lively scene for under-35s; and **The Bowery**, 676 Ann Street (www.thebowery.com.au), for a sophisticated locale and cocktails.

Festivals

Brisbane's top festival is the Brisbane Festival (www.brisbanefestival.com.au), featuring a cultural and entertainment smorgasbord staged over three weeks in September. Brisbane Writers Festival (www.bwf.org.au) brings in renowned international authors. The Brisbane Comedy Festival (www.briscomfest.com) in late February showcases established and up-and-coming Aussie talent and the annual Festival of Classics, sees hundreds of local classical musicians perform around Brisbane. The Brisbane Pride festival (www.brisbanepridefestival.com.au) celebrates gay and lesbian life. The city also hosts touring festivals such as the Future Musical Festival (www.futuremusicfestival.com.au), Soundwave (http://soundwavefestival.com) and St Jerome's Laneway Festival (http://brisbane.lanewayfestival.com).

Outside Brisbane, events include the two-week Cairns Festival (www.festivalcairns.com.au) in August, the not-as-rude-as-it-sounds Festival of the Knob (www.yorkeysknob.com/festival) in Yorkey's Knob every Queen's Birthday weekend (June), and the Woodford Folk Festival (www.woodfordfolkfestival.com), held at the end of December. The Dreaming Festival (www.thedreamingfestival.com) in June – also at Woodford, about hour's drive north of Noosa – celebrates indigenous culture, music and dance.

Surfing off King's Beach on the Sunshine Coast

ACTIVITIES

Queensland's legendary weather and pristine conditions beckon all visitors to join in the fun, whether it is barracking for a football team, barrelling down a wave or floating around a coral garden surrounded by a swirling rainbow of fish.

Australia is famous for its competitive spirit and robust partisanship when it comes to spectator sports, but this is a country of doers, not watchers, and this spirit, coupled with the cracking climate and spectacular coastline, forms a fantastic outdoor playground. The 2011 launch of the Cairns Adventure Festival, which incorporates an Ironman triathlon and running, riding and swimming events open to all, epitomises the participatory approach of the 'Adventurous by Nature' state.

SPECTATOR SPORTS

Four football codes are played in Queensland: rugby league, rugby union, Australian rules and soccer. Rugby League – the most popular – is played at an elite level in the National Rugby League (NRL; www.nrl.com.au) with two Queensland-based teams, the Brisbane Broncos and the North Queensland Cowboys represented. The biggest event in town, however, is when Queensland plays New South Wales in the State of Origin series – fiercely parochial matches. Suncorp Stadium (www.suncorpstadium.com.au; Lang Park, Milton, Brisbane) hosts Queensland's rugby league, rugby union and soccer matches. The Gabba (www.thegabba.org.au; Vulture Street, Woolloongabba, Brisbane) is the home ground of the Brisbane Lions, Queensland's only AFL (Australian Football League) team, and it also hosts major cricket matches.

OUTDOOR ACTIVITIES

Bushwalking
The Queensland government has progressively established walking tracks through some of the most beautiful parts of the state as part of its 'Great Walks' programme. Check out the Queensland Walks website (www.queenslandwalks.com.au) and the Department of National Parks, Recreation, Sport and Racing (www.nprsr.qld.gov.au).

Golf
Queensland has built a reputation for its golf-resort courses, with more than 10 on the Gold Coast and others on the Sunshine Coast and further north near the Whitsundays and Port Douglas. Golf Queensland (www.golfqueensland.org.au) gives info on public-access courses.

On the beach at Port Douglas

Sea kayaking near Cairns

Sailing

Boating enthusiasts are drawn to the 74 islands of the Whitsundays, where even novices are permitted to go 'bareboating' (cruising the calm waters without any crew). Dozens of operators hire yachts and catamarans at Airlie Beach and Shute Harbour. To begin arranging boat charter, see the Whitsunday Tourism website (www.tourismwhitsundays.com) or contact the Whitsunday Central Reservation Centre (tel: 4946 5299).

Sea kayaking and SUPing

Sea kayaking is deservedly popular all over the state, and hundreds of operators, large and small, offer kayak hire and guided paddling tours. See page 70 for one example of a kayaking tour in the Whitsundays. SUP (stand-up paddleboarding – like surfing, but with a paddle) is a relatively new sport that has become enormously popular in Queensland's ideal conditions; it's possible to hire boards in many places.

Surfing

Queensland's surf beaches are concentrated in the southern corner of the state, where there's no reef to interrupt the swell. Surf schools are plentiful – some worth checking out include Cheyne Horan's School of Surf (Surfers Paradise; www.cheynehoran.com.au), Godfathers of the Ocean (Surfers Paradise; www.godfathersoftheocean.com) and Wave Sense (Noosa Heads; www.wavesense.com.au).

Cycling

Humidity and heat aside, cycling in Queensland is fantastic. Cairns was right at the forefront of mountain biking as it evolved as a sport, and Smithfield (the epicentre of MTB in the far north) is a mecca for fat-tyre fans. Cairns is hosting several MTB World Cup events over the next few years, and the World Championships return in 2017. You can hire bikes and ride these trails and a multitude of others around the state. Road riding is popular too. Bicycle Queensland (www.bq.org.au) has information on bicycle-user groups, cycle paths and ride programmes, and the Transport Queensland website (www.transport.qld.gov.au/cycling) also carries information on cycle routes and maps published by local councils from the Gold Coast to Townsville.

Snorkelling and diving

Seeing the Great Barrier Reef up close is a must-do for any visitor to Queensland. Water temperatures stay warm all year round, but August through to January generally offers the best visibility. Scuba-diving in Queensland is highly organised, and a large number of reputable operators offer quality training courses (see page 27). Snorkelling, however, can be just as much fun, with no time limit and almost no cost. Buy or bring your own mask, snorkel and fins, as some places charge a fortune for hire.

Thrills on a Dreamworld rollercoaster

GOLD COAST THEME PARKS

For adrenalin junkies, energetic teens and big kids, the over-the-top theme parks of the Gold Coast provide more than enough exhilaration, glam, glitter and action to occupy a day or three.

Whatever your hobby or obsession, the Gold Coast probably offers it in the form of a 'world' or a theme park. There's Bonsai World, Dreamworld, Frozen World, Sea World, Snooker World, Tropical Fruit World, Warner Brothers Movie World, Whitewater World and the World of Bees to mention just a few, all dishing up folly, fun, fear, fact, fantasy and fast food. Each of them is good value if its product is to your personal taste, or your children's.

The coast's most polished attractions are **Sea World**, **Dreamworld**, **Whitewater World**, **Warner Brothers Movie World** and **Wet 'n' Wild Water World**, all located 15 minutes' drive north of Surfers Paradise on the Gold Coast Highway. The major theme parks offer various joint packages that provide discounted entry to two or more parks, so shop around. Note that last admission to attractions/rides is half an hour before the park closing times given here.

Spit has developed its rides and performances in parallel with a programme of marine animal rescue and welfare that caters for injured whales, dolphins, seals and sea lions.

Shark Bay comprises four large lagoons inhabited by various species of sharks. It is possible for visitors to scuba-dive and snorkel amongst the sharks and touch (very carefully) some of the smaller sea creatures. Another must-see is the **Dolphin Cove Show**, in which these perfectly trained sea mammals join equally well-rehearsed humans in a series of dazzling displays in the world's largest naturalistic lagoon habitat.

More unusually, Sea World also has a polar attraction – **Polar Bear Shores** – in an as-near-to-natural-as-possible Arctic summer environment, created with the use of wind generation, misting and fogging, and rain simulation, as well as natural vegetation.

SEA WORLD

Sea World (Seaworld Drive, Main Beach; www.seaworld.myfun.com.au; daily 10am–5.30pm) on the Southport

DREAMWORLD AND WHITEWATER WORLD

Ever wondered what it feels like to fall backwards off a 38-storey building?

Hollywood Stunt Driver at Warner Brothers Movie World

Dreamworld (Dreamworld Parkway, Coomera; www.dreamworld.com.au; daily 10am–5pm, extended hours during school holidays) provides a pretty good simulation of exactly what that experience would feel like with the **Tower of Terror** ride. The park also offers a sliding scale of less alarming diversions, ranging from the Claw and the Wipeout to rides on rollercoasters, chairlifts, paddle steamers and trains. There is also an IMAX adventure theatre and native (and some international) wildlife, including dingoes, kangaroos and koalas.

Next door, and under the same management, is **Whitewater World** (Dreamworld Parkway, Coomera; www.whitewaterworld.com.au; daily 10am–4pm). Terror, temporary weightlessness, whitewater, plunging, whirlpools and general carnage – that's what you pay your money for here, and that's just during one ride: The Rip.

After that you can check out the massive funnel, the Green Room, and various slides, wave pools and tubes, all of which ensure you get drenched (one ride, rather worryingly, is called 'The Wedgie').

WARNER BROTHERS MOVIE WORLD

Warner Brothers Movie World (Pacific Motorway, Oxenford; www.movieworld.com.au; daily 10am–5.30pm) invites you to enjoy a well-presented, behind-the-scenes view of the illusions involved in movie making. One of its most popular attractions is **Hollywood Stunt Driver**, a simulation of an action movie set with plenty of thrills and spills – all in the best Hollywood tradition. Newer to the line-up is a 3D alien shoot-em-up interactive game called Justice League. It joins an old favourite, Shrek 4-D Adventure Show, with spectacular special effects, and some hair-raising rides, such as the **Batwing Spaceshot** and the **Superman Escape** rollercoaster, where riders are hurled upwards at a speed of 100kph (60mph) and accelerate from 0–100kph in two seconds.

WET 'N' WILD WATER WORLD

Young kids and aquatic thrill-seekers of all ages are well catered for at **Wet 'n' Wild Water World** (Pacific Motorway, Oxenford; www.wetnwild.com.au; daily 10am–4pm, later in summer). Younger children can head to **Buccaneer Bay**, while older adrenalin junkies will love **Extreme H2O Zone** with its huge slides and high-speed rides, including the Black Hole – a tube slide that sends you spiralling through utter darkness.

Other slightly more sedate highlights in the park are the **Giant Wave Pool** and a 15-minute tube ride along a slow-moving river from the simulated tropical island's **Calypso Beach**.

Learning to dive

GREAT BARRIER REEF

The Great Barrier Reef, a protected World Heritage Area, is one of the most beautiful and diverse natural phenomena in the world, and its full wonder and glory are accessible to anyone who can don a mask and snorkel.

The Great Barrier Reef, one of the Seven Natural Wonders of the World, is an aquatic wilderness bigger than the UK, Holland and Switzerland put together. The reef extends over 250,000 sq km (96,500 sq miles) and comprises some 3,000 individual coral reefs and 940 islands running along the Queensland coast from north of Cape York Peninsula to just north of Fraser Island.

Declared a World Heritage Area in 1981, it is an extraordinarily complex ecosystem, a dazzlingly beautiful universe of low-wooded islands, mangrove estuaries, sea-grass beds, algae and sponge gardens, sandy and coral cays, mud floors and deep ocean troughs.

The largest structure built by living organisms on earth, the reef contains one-third of the known species of soft corals and more than 360 hard corals. It is also the home of 1,500 species of fish, dugongs, marine turtles, dolphins, whales, sea snakes, birds and sharks.

WHEN TO SEE THE REEF

The weather will play an important part in your experience of the reef. From late April through to October it is at its best,

the clear skies and moderate breezes offering perfect conditions for coral-viewing, snorkelling, diving and swimming. In November the first signs of the approaching 'wet' appear: variable winds, increasing cloud and showers. By January it rains at least once most days.

Even in winter the water is never cold, but it's worth paying a couple of dollars extra to hire a wetsuit anyway; most people find it hard not to go on snorkelling for hours in this extraordinary environment.

November to May is stinger (jellyfish) season in North Queensland. Although not considered a great risk when swimming on the outer reefs, stingers are potentially deadly, and stinger suits can act as a preventative measure and also offer great protection from the sun. Stinger suits should be offered to guests on diving and snorkelling trips, sometimes for hire, sometimes for free.

HOW TO SEE THE REEF

One of the easiest ways to visit the reef is to take a day trip from Cairns, Port Douglas, Airlie Beach or Cape Tribulation. Almost all day trips follow a similar format: a morning dive, followed by

Exploring Osprey Reef   *Reef sharks*

a buffet lunch, then, assuming you've not eaten too much or partaken of free beer, an afternoon dive. There should be a marine biologist on board, who will explain the reef's ecology. Before you book, also ask about the number of passengers the boat takes; this varies from several hundred to fewer than a dozen on smaller craft.

Learn to dive

While snorkelling the reef satisfies many, you might want to learn to dive to maximise your experience. Recommended dive schools in Queensland include: Deep Sea Divers Den (www.dlversden. com.au); Prodive Cairns (www.prodive cairns.com), Reef Safari (www.reef safari.com),and Tusa Dive (www.tusa dive.com). These provide dive courses as well as organised dive trips (see page 23). For more, visit www.padi.com.

Day-trip operators

By no means a comprehensive list, the following operators run day trips to the reef. **Great Adventures** (Reef Fleet Terminal, 1 Spence Street, Cairns; www. greatadventures.com.au) runs several options to Green Island, only 45 minutes from Cairns, as well as to a pontoon on the outer reef with semi-submersibles and underwater observatory. Also in Cairns, **Reef Magic** (Reef Fleet Terminal, 1 Spence Street; www.reefmagic. com.au) offers the chance to spend five hours at their Marine World pontoon at Moore Reef, with semi-submersible,

optional guided snorkelling tours and helicopter flights. **Cruise Whitsundays** (www.cruisewhitsundays.com), operating out of Hamilton Island, offer days trips to ReefWorld, a pontoon where introductory dives are conducted by **Reef Safari** (www.reefsafari.com).

The wave-piercing catamarans of **Quicksilver Cruises** (Marina Mirage; www.quicksilver-cruises.com/diving) based in Port Douglas, speed out to a floating platform at Agincourt Reef with an underwater observatory and semi-submersible vessel.

Cruises and live-aboard vessels

Live-aboard vessels provide fully catered voyages where you overnight at sea to maximise the time spent on the reef. Voyages usually range from three to seven days, and the price includes all meals, entertainment and activities. Usually, but not exclusively, catering to experienced divers, live-aboard trips offer dive instructors and/or marine biologists along with the benefits of small-group touring. One of the most experienced and best operators is **Mike Ball Dive Expeditions** (www.mikeball.com; 3 Abbott Street, Cairns), which runs three- to 10-day cruises departing from Cairns.

Great Barrier Reef islands

Numerous continental islands and coral cays within the Great Barrier Reef region offer resort accommodation, from camping to luxury. The following is a small selection:

Deep-sea divers

Green Island (www.greenislandresort. com.au). A coral cay with an eco-sensitive resort. A popular day-trip destination from Cairns.

Hamilton Island (www.hamiltonisland. com.au). The major resort island in the Whitsunday group, accessed from Airlie Beach, with numerous accommodation and tour options.

Heron Island (www.heronisland.com). Accessed via Gladstone, a coral cay with one boutique resort and miles of coral reef.

Fitzroy Island (www.fitzroyisland.com) A short hop from Cairns, with a newly reopened resort, lots of good snorkelling, a turtle hospital and a PADI dive centre.

Lizard Island (www.lizardisland.com.au). A remote continental island, accessed by air from Cairns, with access to the famous Cod Hole and Osprey Reef dive sites, and a five-star resort.

Magnetic Island (www.magnetic-island.com.au). A delightfully unpretentious island, accessed by sea from Townsville, with several budget and mid-range accommodation and tour options.

Orpheus Island (www.orpheusisland. com). Out-of-the-way Orpheus is a luxurious retreat with just 21 communication-technology-free guest rooms. Access is by air from Townsville or Cairns.

EXPERIENCING THE REEF

Every morning, dozens of state-of-the-art dive boats and wave-piercing cata- marans head out from Cairns and Port Douglas to the outer reef. About an hour later, regardless of their departure point, they will be moored over the coral. Because the water is so shallow, snorkelling is a perfectly satisfactory way of experiencing the brilliant colours of the reef and marine life. Many people prefer it to the more technical scuba-diving; even so, most boats offer tanks for experienced divers and 'resort dives' for people who have never dived before.

As soon as you poke your head underwater, the world erupts. It's almost sensory overload: there are vast forests of staghorn coral, whose tips glow purple like electric Christmas-tree lights; brilliant-blue clumps of mushroom coral; layers of pink plate coral; and bulbous green brain coral. Tropical fish slip about, showing off their fluorescent patterns: painted flutemouth, long-finned batfish, crimson squirrel fish and hump-headed Maori wrasse. You should not interfere with any of the life on the reef, which is why buoyancy control is so important, and definitely do not touch a poisonous barbed stonefish.

The course of Australian history might have been very different had Commander James Cook been less fortunate when his ship *The Endeavour* ran aground on the reef in June 1770. By jettisoning a load of heavy cargo his crew managed to repair the ship and return to sea, but not all seafarers have been so lucky; 30 shipwrecks lie in the

Snorkellers by their dive boat   *Green Island is easy to reach from Cairns*

reef's waters and experienced divers will enjoy exploring them.

Flying is an alternative way to experience the reef, and from the air you can often spot migrating whales and sea turtles. **Cairns Seaplanes** (www.cairnsseaplanes.com) offers several tours combining a landing at Green Island and the chance to snorkel the reef.

THREATS TO THE REEF

In December 2013, the Australian government controversially gave the go ahead for increased industrial activity around the Great Barrier Reef, in a decision that paved the way for dredging and dumping to occur within the World Heritage-listed area. The dredging is to give big tankers access to Abbot Point, which will also see a large increase in the shipping traffic passing through the reef. The decision – taken only a few years after a Chinese tanker ran aground on the reef, tearing a huge gash in the coral and hemorrhaging thousands of litres of oil into the fragile eco system – has drawn widespread horror and condemnation from conservation groups, environmental agencies and the general public at home and abroad, and has led to concerns that UNESCO will label Great Barrier Reef as endangered.

Other major threats to the health of the reef include coral bleaching. If the clear, tropical waters remain too warm for too long, corals expel their photosynthesising zooxanthellae and become colourless. Bleached corals are not necessarily dead and can regain their original algae if not too stressed, but if the water doesn't cool within about a month the coral will die. Up to five percent of the Great Barrier Reef has been severely damaged during each of the last two major bleaching events; increased temperatures from global warming are thought to be implicated.

Corals are also damaged by boat anchors, sewage from resorts, and by divers and snorkellers. The dugong and all six of the reef's marine turtle species are threatened because of the loss and degradation of their habitat.

When the Europeans settled, they cleared forests, mined, engaged in agriculture and established towns. Coastal wetland forest is still being cut down to make room for the beef cattle, sugar cane, cotton industries and banana plantations close to the coast. Hundreds of reefs are at risk from the sediment and chemical run-off from farming, and from the loss of the coastal wetlands that have acted as a natural filter in the past.

About a fifth of Queensland's population lives along the coast adjacent to the reef, and with the current interstate and overseas migration to the state (over 200 people each day), communities continue to grow. How to manage water quality, tourism and commercial and recreational fishing is a major concern.

Tugging a cargo ship in Brisbane Harbour, 1891

HISTORY: KEY DATES

Aborigines lived in Queensland for 50,000 years before the arrival of Captain Cook. An energetic population – explorers, emancipated convicts and free settlers – carved out a life here. Today, the Gold Coast is the nation's fastest-growing region.

BEFORE THE EUROPEANS

c.50,000 BC Humans arrive in Australia from eastern Asia via New Guinea, travelling on foot.

THE FIRST EUROPEANS

1770 On 22 August Captain James Cook, aboard the *Endeavour*, raises the Union flag on Possession Island, Cape York, and claims eastern Australia for King George III.

1799 Explorer Matthew Flinders names Redcliffe Point, which becomes the site of Queensland's first European settlement.

1824 First convicts and jailers arrive at Redcliffe, on Moreton Bay.

1831 Convict population peaks at 947.

1842 Brisbane is declared open for free settlement.

1846 Schooner *Coolangatta* wrecked. Brisbane becomes a port of entry.

1848 Queensland's first immigrant ship, *Artemisia*, reaches Moreton Bay.

STATEHOOD

1859 Statehood comes with separation from NSW and the naming of Queensland (European population 23,520).

1860s Sugar planted at Redland Bay, providing a ready source of rum.

1887 Brisbane connected by rail to Sydney. Difficulties (which still exist) arise because of Queensland's choice of narrow gauge, which did not match that of the southern states.

1901 On 1 January Australia's six independent colonies are federated into the Commonwealth of Australia.

The procession of the 41st Battalion through Brisbane on Anzac Day 1916

WAR AND BOOMTIME

1914	Australian troops join the allies in World War I.
1915	On 25 April, ANZAC troops begin the Gallipoli campaign in Turkey, which results in major loss of life.
1933	Surfers Paradise township is named after hotelier James Cavill's hotel of the same name.
1939	Outbreak of World War II: Australian forces fight in Europe and the Middle East. Later in the war, Australia's military forces fight the Japanese in the Pacific theatre.
1941	First convoy of US servicemen arrives in Brisbane, which becomes a large military base.
1959	The city of The Gold Coast is established.
1974	Cyclone Wanda crosses the coast. Brisbane's worst flood since 1893.
1982	The 12th Commonwealth Games held in Brisbane.
1988	Australia celebrates its bicentenary. Brisbane hosts World Expo '88.
1992	Australian High Court rejects *Terra Nullus* (empty land) concept; theoretically great swathes of Crown Land could be claimed by Aboriginal groups under Native Title law.

21ST CENTURY

From 2000	Fed by immigration from the south, Queensland's population is grows at twice the national rate.
2005	Brisbane launches its long-range bid for the 2024 Olympics.
2007	Brisbane's Gallery of Modern Art (GoMa), Australia's largest contemporary art space, opens its doors.
2011	In January the Brisbane area floods, killing 38 people, and three quarters of the state of Queensland is declared a disaster zone. In February, Severe Tropical Cyclone Yasi leaves a trail of carnage across northern Queensland.
2011	Cairns Adventure Festival launched, incorporating an Ironman triathlon and numerous other events.
2013–14	Australian government approves increased shipping and industrial activity within Great Barrier Reef Marine Park, sparking environmental concerns about the future of the reef.

BEST ROUTES

Story Bridge at night

BRISBANE CITY CENTRE

This stroll around Brisbane's Central Business District (CBD) unveils Queensland's colonial history, showcases architectural landmarks and taps into the bustle of one of Australia's fastest growing cities. On the way, discover its wild and natural corners, shopping bazaars and dining scene.

DISTANCE: 6km (3.75 miles)
TIME: A half-day
START: Riverside Centre
END: Brisbane Arcade
POINTS TO NOTE: Let the weather influence your pace and timing on this walking route and remember your sunscreen, hat and water. Along the way there are numerous places to buy a drink and catch some breeze in the shade by the river. Although there is one hill, the steep climb comes early on in the tour, and overall it is not a particularly strenuous walk.

As it meanders towards the coast, Queensland's longest river, the Brisbane, makes a deep loop around Spring Hill, the location of Brisbane's CBD and the heart of the city. This part of town lies about 20km (12 miles) upstream from where the river empties into Moreton Bay.

An excellent introduction to Brisbane is the City Sights bus tour (www.citysights.com.au). Buses leave every 45 minutes from 19 stops, with the first bus leaving Post Office Square at 9am and the last bus departing from there at 3.45pm. There's informative commentary, and you can hop off and hop on a following bus to explore at your own pace. Your ticket permits same-day travel on CityCat ferry services.

Historical development

To the indigenous Yuggera people, this mangrove-lined bend in the river was a traditional fishing ground and the location of a crossing point known as Min-an-jin.

The Moreton Bay penal settlement – the last major port to be established in the colony of what was then New South Wales – was founded in 1824 for the resettlement of repeat offenders from Sydney. Initially located at Redcliffe, in in 1825 the settlement was moved to North Quay, the site of the present-day CBD to improve security and gain access to a reliable supply of fresh water: the spring-fed creeks running off Spring Hill. In 1842 Britain closed the Moreton Bay penal settlement and declared the area open to free settlers. Private enterprise soon

Anzac Square   *Commissariat Store*

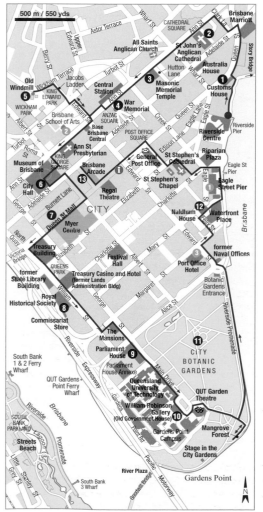

grasped the opportunities for growth, and the settlement's population grew to almost 6,000 by the time Queensland became a self-governing colony in 1859, with Brisbane anointed as its capital.

Today's bustling city barely has time to acknowledge its past, as new skyscrapers continue to vie for the title of Brisbane's tallest. Perhaps a late developer compared to its southern siblings, Brisbane is now making up for lost time and shows no sign of slowing down or looking back.

BRISBANE RIVER

Start from the architecturally acclaimed highrise **Riverside Centre** and **Riparian Plaza**, which dominate the Riverside Precinct. Have breakfast at the **Groove Train**, see ❶, where you can watch the CityCat ferries beetle under Story Bridge (see page 38) to disgorge well dressed commuters at the pier. Also look out for climbers on the top girders of Story

Customs House

Bridge – if you would like to join them, check out Story Bridge Adventure Climb (www.sbac.net.au).

CUSTOMS HOUSE

Head north (downstream) along the Riverside Promenade and after a few hundred metres the stately, copper-domed **Customs House ❶** comes into view. This colonnaded example of Victorian architecture was constructed in 1886–9; it is now owned by the University of Queensland and provides an interesting visual contrast to the glass skyscrapers towering behind. Climb the well-worn sandstone stairs to emerge on Queen Street. The impressive 1888 facade opposite is what remains of a warehouse, indicating, along with the Customs House itself, the significance of river trade during the boom-time of the late 1800s.

Turn right and walk along Queen Street to the intersection with Adelaide Street. Cross here and ascend the narrow Clark Lane to Ann Street and turn left.

ST JOHN'S CATHEDRAL

Ann Street boasts several significant religious buildings, but taking pride of place is the Gothic Revival **St John's Anglican Cathedral ❷** with its soaring steeple at No. 373. The foundation stone was laid in 1901, but construction continued on and off for over 100 years. Architecture buffs will be excited by Australia's only example of a vaulted ceiling constructed entirely of stone.

Continue southwest down Ann Street. Just past Hutton Lane on the left is the impressive facade of the **Masonic Memorial Temple ❸** (No. 311; tours Mon–Fri 2pm; free) with its four-storey-high columns. Built in 1930, the temple has a striking Grand Hall and Grand Foyer.

ANZAC SQUARE

Keep walking downhill along Ann Street and cross Creek Street. The clock tower of **Central Station** is soon on your right, and directly opposite is the poignant **ANZAC Square War Memorial and Parkland ❹**. The **Shrine of Remembrance** features an eternal flame and 18 columns representing 1918, the year that peace was declared after World War I. Beneath is an underpass to Central Station and a **World War II Shrine of Memories** (Mon–Fri 9am–2.15pm; free).

Cross over Ann Street to Central Station, and continue towards the Edward Street intersection. On the corner diagonally opposite is the elaborate Base Brisbane Central hostel building, which was built for the Salvation Army in 1911.

KING EDWARD PARK

Turn right at Edward Street, and climb the hill to cross over Turbot Street and

George Street's Mansions   *The Old Windmill*

enter **King Edward Park**. The entrance to the park is guarded by three striking bronze sculptures looking like props from a sci-fi movie. Panels reveal they are actually sets from a classical play, *Agamemnon*. Behind the sculptures, the bright red steps of **Jacobs Ladder** lead you towards **Spring Hill** and the high point of this walk. Turn left at the top of the stairs and head towards the **Old Windmill** ❺. Established in 1828, this modest structure is Queensland's oldest surviving building. Its dubious effectiveness as a windmill led to the introduction of a treadmill, an instrument of punishment with the power being provided by unruly convicts. Retrace your footsteps back along Edward Street, and turn right to go southwest along Ann Street.

KING GEORGE SQUARE

About 50m/yds from the corner is **Bleeding Heart**, see ❷, a breakfast, lunch and coffee stop set in the Brisbane School of Arts building. Continue along Ann Street until you reach **King George Square** at the confluence of Ann and Albert streets. **Brisbane City Hall** ❻ dominates this expansive public space and hosts the **Museum of Brisbane** (www.museumofbrisbane.com.au; daily 10am–5pm; free), which features displays revealing the history of Brisbane, as well as contemporary art. Take a lift up City Hall's bell tower for stupendous views; afterwards, stroll

south through the square to cross Adelaide Street and walk one block back to Albert Street.

Queen Street Mall ❼ is pedestrianised between Edward and George streets and hosts a multitude of shopping and eating possibilities (see page 39). For now, continue southwest, crossing George Street towards the Treasury Building.

WILLIAM STREET

Continue southwest alongside the Italianate **Treasury Building**, which houses a 24-hour casino behind its numerous arches, and turn left down William Street. Stroll through Queens Park with its stern statue of Queen Victoria and pass by the grand Lands Administration Building, now the **Treasury Casino and Hotel** (see page 102). On the opposite side of the road is the **Commissariat Store** ❽ (No. 115; Tue–Fri 10am–4pm; free), an 1829 convict-era building housing a museum focusing on Brisbane's earliest beginnings and local Aboriginal history.

PARLIAMENT HOUSE

Cross back to the eastern side of William Street and head southeast to Margaret Street and turn left. Turn right on George Street passing **The Mansions**, charming three-storey terraced housing, on the way to **Parliament House** ❾ (corner George and Alice streets; www.

Detail on Brisbane City Hall

parliament.qld.gov.au; Mon–Fri 9am–4.30, Sat–Sun 10am–2pm; free), where there are on-demand guided tours of the fully restored interior and decorative antiques. Alternatively, observe all the action (or boredom) from the visitors' gallery when parliament sits (see website).

Resume your walk south past the lush Botanic Gardens on your left and the **Queensland University of Technology** (QUT) on your right. Soon a sweeping driveway on your right heralds the presence of the serene, creamy-stone **Old Government House** ❿ (2 George Street; www.ogh.qut.edu.au; Sun–Fri 10am–5pm; free). Once the home of Queensland's governors, the attractive mansion also houses the exceptional **William Robinson Gallery**, filled with the work of this award-winning Queensland artist.

CITY BOTANIC GARDENS

Cross over George Street, past the QUT Gardens Theatre and enter the **City Botanic Gardens** ⓫ (daily, 24 hours; free). Originally a convict-worked farm, the gardens were formally laid out in 1855 – now you can explore them (and go much further) by hiring a bike from nearby Bike Obsession (133 Mary Street; www.bikeobsession.com.au; Mon–Fri 7.30am–5.30pm, Sat–Sun 10am–3pm; charge).

Consider pausing at the café for refreshments, then head down the stone steps through rainforest towards the river. At the Riverside Promenade, turn right where you will see a boardwalk extending out into the **mangrove forest**. Follow the boardwalk looking for birdlife and read about the significance of the muddy mangrove ecosystem on panels. Rejoin the promenade and head north.

EDWARD STREET TO EAGLE STREET

Exit the gardens at Edward Street passing the old **Naval Offices**, now occupied by upmarket boutiques and restaurants, on your right. On the corner with Margaret Street is the **Port Office Hotel**, see ❸, a popular lunch option. Turn right at Margaret Street and then left along Felix Street. At the Mary Street intersection, turn right beside the colonial **Naldham House** ⓬. When you reach the anchor beside the eastern wall, turn around. Three small brass plaques on the corner of the building mark the water levels of the 1893, 1896 and 1974 floods. Can't see the 1893 plaque? Look up!

Pass under the shade sails towards the river and the **Eagle Street Pier** complex. Here you'll find more eateries and cafés, plus paddle-steamer cruise boats (www.kookaburrariverqueens.com) and a ferry terminal. If you're looking for a detour, hop on a stubby river ferry from the Eagle Street Pier to Holman Street on Kangaroo Point and check out the charismatic **Story**

In Queen Street Mall

The grand structure of Brisbane's City Hall

Bridge Hotel. The ferry ride affords great views of the city and Story Bridge, particularly at night. Turn right outside the Holman Street terminal and follow the riverside walkway for 500m/yds as far as Bright Street. Turn left and you will spot the Story Bridge Hotel (see page 122) tucked under the Story Bridge approach ramp.

BACK TO QUEEN STREET MALL

To continue with this route, head west, away from the river, to the intersection of Creek, Eagle and Charlotte streets. Walk southwest along Charlotte Street towards the steps leading up to the beautifully refurbished **St Stephen's Cathedral** (entrance on Elizabeth Street) dating from the 1860s, and the neighbouring **St Stephen's Chapel**, Queensland's first church, built in 1850.

Cross Elizabeth Street in front of the cathedral and take the narrow lane between Brisbane GPO and Newspaper House (now the Manor Apartment Hotel) to emerge on Queen Street with the open plaza of **Post Office Square** opposite. Turn left on Queen Street and cross over Edward Street to enter Queen Street Mall. Pass by the helpful **Brisbane Visitor Information Centre** (Queen Street Mall; tel: 3006 6290; www.visitbrisbane.com.au; daily 9am–5pm) and walk 400m/yds until you reach **Brisbane Arcade** ⑱ on your right. The three storeys of the arcade, which runs through to Adelaide Street, are crammed with tempting elegant tearooms, jewellers and high-end fashion shops.

Food and Drink

① GROOVE TRAIN

Riparian Plaza, 123 Eagle Street; tel: 3220 0420; www.groovetrain.com.au; daily 7.30am–late; $$

Enjoy a cup of Veneziano coffee, freshly roasted in Brisbane's West End, chased down with eye-popping views of the Story Bridge and Kangaroo Point, and a bowl of seasonal fruits (or baked eggs and chorizo).

② BLEEDING HEART

166 Ann Street; tel: 3229 0395; www.bleedingheart.com.au; Mon–Fri 7.30am–5pm; $$

The deep and beautiful verandas of the sandstone School of Arts building shelter this charming gallery and café with fairtrade coffee and tea and refreshing ice-cream sodas. Try the ginger beer ice-cream soda while relaxing on the elevated veranda.

③ PORT OFFICE HOTEL

Corner Margaret and Edward streets; tel: 3003 4700; www.portofficehotel.com.au; Mon–Sat 11.30am–9pm; $$–$$$

Choose between a good-value bar meal in the casual Marble Bar, tapas in the Fix Bar or elegant dining in the Fix Restaurant. There are wood-fired pizzas, vegetarian dishes and seafood, though the steaks enjoy pride of place.

Enjoying the South Bank Parklands

BRISBANE SOUTH BANK

Filled with entertainment and dining options and wrapped in green parklands, South Bank is Brisbane's playground and Queensland's premier cultural precinct. The area is designed just as much for strolls and relaxation as it is for showcasing its various edifying and recreational attractions.

DISTANCE: 3.75km (2.5 miles) walk; 5km (3-mile) CityCat ride
TIME: A leisurely full day
START: Goodwill Bridge
END: South Bank Wharf 1
POINTS TO NOTE: This walk starts on the CBD side of the Brisbane River, near the City Botanic Gardens, and crosses the river on the car-free Goodwill Bridge. You can return to the CBD by the same bridge, or the solar-powered Kurilpa footbridge, or by Victoria Bridge, but the CityCat (www.translink.com.au/ferries) affords a more relaxing return trip with great views, and delivers you to the Riverside Precinct, a locality crammed with restaurants.

South Bank was developed for the 1988 World Expo, and as such it is an outstanding example of the positive legacy such large public events can bestow on cities. This former industrial wasteland now has something for everyone: bring your bathers for a splash at Streets Beach, your head for heights for a spin on the Wheel of Brisbane, and your sense of adventure for the Gallery of Modern Art.

Begin at the **Goodwill Bridge ❶** on Gardens Point near the southwest corner of the City Botanic Gardens (see page 38), close to the outdoor **Riverstage**. Built in 2001, this bridge takes its name from Brisbane's Goodwill Games held in the same year. A small coffee stand, Caffe sul Ponte, serving good espresso, is parked on the bridge towards this end.

QUEENSLAND MARITIME MUSEUM

At the other end of the bridge, a tugboat, a warship and a very odd-looking lightship (half-lighthouse, half-ship) announce the **Queensland Maritime Museum ❷** (Stanley Street; www.maritimemuseum.com.au; daily 9.30am–4.30pm, last entry at 3.30pm; charge). Since Dutch explorers landed on Cape York Peninsula in 1606, the sea has shaped Queenslanders' lives and commerce, and this museum focuses on the state's close links with the sea and historical dependence on it.

HMAS Diamantina   *Kurilpa Bridge*

SOUTH BANK

Opposite the museum you will see the entrance to the **Arbour**, a bougainvillea-draped archway of metal tendrils and wire supports. This living art form shelters a path that meanders through the South Bank Parklands as far as the Wheel of Brisbane (see page 42).

Heading northwest along the Arbour you pass between shady picnic grounds and the Boardwalk, the first of the Arbour's several restaurant zones. A small formal garden appears on your right with a statue of Confucius, where the Arbour swings around a cluster of cafés.

Stanley Street Plaza

Where the cafés end, the **Stanley Street Plaza** ❸ begins. A usually quiet public space featuring the **South Bank Visitor Centre** (South Bank House, Corner of Ernest and Stanley Street Plaza; daily 9am–5pm), the plaza comes alive with buskers and market-goers at the weekend as the venue for the **Collective Markets** (www.collectivemarkets.com.au; Sat 10am–9pm, Sun 9am–4pm). Stalls sell all manner of unique items, from craft collectables to chilli sauces, sarongs to sombreros.

Little Stanley Street

Parallel to the plaza and bordering the parklands, Little Stanley Street is packed with bars and quality restaurants offering casual sidewalk dining. Even if you are not yet hungry, check out what's on offer for future reference. The range of cuisine served up is extraordinary, and includes the exotic ambience and Turkish cuisine of **Ahmet's**, see ❶, and the modern Asian flavours of **Obsession Restaurant** (see page 42).

Streets Beach to the Wheel

Between Stanley Street Plaza and the river is **Streets Beach** ❹ (daily; free), Australia's only city-bound beach. This man-made lagoon, complete with sandy shore and lifesavers, is a surreal sight with a muddy river and city skyline as a backdrop, but with no waves or dangerous rips and plenty of shady palm trees, it is one of South Bank's most popular attractions.

North of the beach, the Arbour weaves between clusters of cafés and

Food and Drink

❶ AHMET'S

10/168 Grey Street; tel: 3846 6699; www.ahmets.com; daily 11.30am–3pm, Sun–Thur 5–9pm, Fri–Sat 5–10pm; $$
Be transported to a vibrant bazaar in this colourfully atmospheric Turkish restaurant. Attention to detail extends to the dishes, best shared, which are simply delicious. Dive into the dips, but leave room for the spicy lamb *pide* or the delicious *guvec* (casserole). Entry is from both Grey and Little Stanley streets.

Strolling in the South Bank Parklands

restaurants and the Suncorp Piazza, a well-used concert venue that often also screens sporting events or movies for free. Take the **Rainforest Walk**, where you should spot a water dragon, a striking yet harmless lizard. The boardwalk emerges at the intricately carved **Nepalese Pagoda**, constructed for the 1988 World Expo.

Towering almost 60 metre (197ft) above the parklands, the **Wheel of Brisbane** ❺ (www.thewheelofbrisbane.com.au; charge) is worth a spin. You receive geographical and historical commentary while inside your air-conditioned pod.

QUEENSLAND CULTURAL CENTRE

Much of Queensland's celebration of culture culminates in this assemblage of edifices at the northern end of the South Bank Parklands. As you leave the Wheel of Brisbane, walk north along the Cultural Forecourt. On your left is the

Queensland Performing Arts Centre (QPAC) ❻ (corner Grey and Melbourne streets; www.qpac.com.au). With a multitude of theatres, galleries and event spaces, there is always some action here. (Check out www.visitsouthbank.com.au for a full events calendar and detailed information on all attractions and shows, at the QPAC and beyond.)

Turn left to skirt the northern side of QPAC, where lifts and stairs lead to a walkway over Melbourne Street and to the **Queensland Museum** ❼ (corner Grey and Melbourne streets; www.southbank.qm.qld.gov.au; daily 9am–5pm; free). This compact, well-laid-out museum succinctly explores Queensland's natural and social history. The Museum Zoo is a creative line-up of stuffed critters where you can compare your own size and physical abilities against members of the animal kingdom. There is also a kid-friendly, hands-on **Sciencentre** (9.30am–5pm; charge).

The striking Queensland State Library

Two galleries

Exit the museum where you entered. On your left, the **Whale Mall** reverberates to the recordings of humpback whales; look up to see life-size recreations of these mammals. Straight ahead is a passage heading towards the river and the **Queensland Art Gallery** ❽ (Stanley Place; www.qag.qld.gov.au; daily 10am–5pm; free). Head along the passage and find the entrance on the river side of the gallery. Inside, visiting exhibitions accompany indigenous, classical and contemporary art from Australia and abroad, particularly Asia and the Pacific region.

Exit the gallery from the northern side and walk across the elevated plaza over Peel Street towards the **Queensland State Library** (www.slq.qld.gov.au; daily 10am–5pm, to 8pm Mon–Thur). Pass through the centre of the library via the sheltered Knowledge Walk, where you can take advantage of free Wi-fi. This ground-floor walkway opens out onto a compound facing the dramatic, glass and steel **Gallery of Modern Art (GoMA)** ❾ (same contact details as the Queensland Art Gallery; free). The light-filled modern space showcases contemporary art in a variety of media.

KURILPA BRIDGE

Northeast of GoMA, a lawn descends to the Riverside Boardwalk. To the north, **Kurilpa Bridge**, a sculptural (and controversial) structure of steel masts and cables, with solar-powered LED lighting, is a bridge for pedestrians and cyclists that connects South Bank with the CBD. If your accommodation is in the north of the city this would be the quick way back to base. Otherwise, turn south and follow the boardwalk under Victoria Bridge back to **South Bank Wharf 1**. Here you can catch a CityCat ferry and cruise past Gardens Point to the Riverside Centre.

MORETON ISLAND

Moreton Island, just a short ferry trip from Brisbane, delivers a great action-packed day. Four-wheel driving along its vast sandy beaches, plunging into a pristine blue lagoon, snorkelling among shipwrecks, and hand-feeding wild dolphins are just a few of the adventures on offer.

DISTANCE: 50km (31 miles)
TIME: A full day
START/END: Tangalooma Island Resort
POINTS TO NOTE: You will need a 4WD vehicle for this trip, either hired in Brisbane (see page 134) or pre-booked from Tangalooma Resort (see page 135). The route, with stops, will take approximately four hours. The Tangalooma Launch departs at 7am and 10am from Holt Street Wharf (arrive 30 mins early); the resort also offers coach transfers (charge) from city hotels for the 10am launch. Vehicles take the MiCat barge (14 Howard Smith Drive; www.moretonislandadventures. com.au; Mon, Wed, Thur and Sat 8.30am, Fri 8.30am and 1pm, Sun 8.30 and 2.30pm) from the Port of Brisbane. You will need a vehicle access permit (charge) from the MiCat barge or from the Department of National Parks, Recreation, Sports and Racing (NPRSR; http://parks.nprsr.qld.gov.au/permits/). Book accommodation ahead at Tangalooma Resort.

Until the early 1960s, Tangalooma on Moreton Island was one of the world's largest whaling stations, operating from 1951 to 1962, conveniently located close to a narrow deep-water channel, along which about 10,000 humpback whales migrated every year. It was estimated that just 500 humpbacks remained ten years after the station was established. Soon after, the authorities put a stop to all whaling from Tangalooma.

Today, Moreton Island is over 95 percent National Park, and is home to just three small villages and Tangalooma Island Resort. The latter now occupies the whaling station site and whales remain one Tangalooma's main attractions between June and November, when the humpbacks perform spectacular tail and flipper slapping and giant breaches.

TANGALOOMA ISLAND RESORT

Tangalooma Island Resort ❶ (tel: 3637 2000; www.tangalooma.com) offers several dining options, a general store, an ATM and numerous land- and water-based activities, as well as accom-

Tangalooma Island Resort

modation – it is very expensive to hire snorkelling gear, however, so bring your own if possible. Unless you have driven to the island, this is where you will pick up your pre-booked 4WD. Before you head off, grab a snack and drink from the **Beach Café**, see ❶.

Follow signs to the track that leads onto the beach (there is a no-driving zone in front of the resort): from here the drive

Feeding the dolphins

will be entirely on sand. Note that the best and safest time for beach driving is two hours either side of low tide; tide charts are provided with the island driving permit or the resort vehicle hire. To start, head north just past the Tangalooma Wrecks and turn right onto the inland track, Middle Road.

BLUE LAGOON

After 7km (4 miles) you will reach the eastern side of the island. Turn left and head north along this beautiful 38km (23-mile) stretch of ocean beach. After 8km (5 miles), leave the beach to visit the **Blue Lagoon ❷**, the island's largest freshwater lake, where white sandy shores are lapped by gin-clear water.

CAPE MORETON

A further 8km (5 miles) north is the tip of **Cape Moreton ❸**, where stunning 360-degree views stretch to the Glass House Mountains, on the mainland, and to North Stradbroke Island. You can sit and watch marine wildlife below while enjoying a picnic lunch: turtles, dolphins, sharks, whales, rays and schools of fish are commonly spotted.

The 1.5km (1-mile) walk around the headland (the only part of the island that is not pure sand) winds past the **Cape Moreton Lighthouse**, the oldest operating lighthouse in Queensland and an important navigation aid to all ships entering the bay. It was built in 1857 with

sandstone blocks quarried by 35 prisoners. The unmanned **Moreton Island National Park Information Centre** near the lighthouse provides details on the island's history and wildlife.

Return to the car park and continue west on the inland track, which briefly returns to the beach past **Yellow Patch**, a large dark yellow sand blow (drifting dunes created when denuded of vegetation). The track then veers inland once again to bypass several tidal lagoons.

BULWER AND COWAN COWAN

Back on the western side of the island, the route passes behind the tiny settlements of Bulwer and Cowan Cowan. (The beaches in front of these two small communities are closed to traffic.) On the beach at **Bulwer ❹**, three hulks lie on the sand, having been originally scuttled and placed there in the 1930s to form a safe anchorage for small boats. Some 5.5km (3.5 miles) further south, **Cowan Cowan ❺** is the site of Fort Cowan, an old navy signal station that was Brisbane's first line of defence during World War II.

TANGALOOMA WRECKS

It is only a short drive now along the beach to one of the island's most recognisable landmarks – the **Tangalooma Wrecks ❻**. In total, 15 ships that once sailed around Australia have been scuttled here to form a small-craft anchorage. *The Maryborough*, an iron-hulled bucket

Tangalooma wrecks

Sand tobagganing

dredge built in 1885, was the first to be scuttled in July 1963. The wrecks are perfect for snorkelling and scuba-diving. Guided snorkelling trips are offered by Tangalooma Water Sports & Diveworld.

TANGALOOMA ACTIVITIES

It is now time to return to Tangalooma Island Resort, where thrill-seekers can chose from a range of afternoon activities, including quadbike rides in the dunes, jet ski rides, parasailing and seasonal whale-watching cruises. The **Desert Safari Tour** (four daily, 1.5 hours duration; charge) includes a 4WD bus tour through the bush to 'the desert'. This is in fact a 42ha (100-acre) sandblow.

The huge dunes are the venue for **sand tobogganing**; a flimsy piece of waxed board is all you need to fly down at exhilarating speeds of about 60kph (40mph).

After all that you might want some sustenance. The resort has a couple of good (seasonal) restaurants including the **Tursiops Buffet Restaurant**, see ❷, with two new spots, **Fire and Stone**, due to open soon at time of writing.

A 4WD hired from Tangalooma will need to be returned by 5pm. There is a 4pm launch back to the mainland, but a better option is to stay for dolphin-feeding at sunset, and return to Brisbane on the 7pm launch.

Bottlenose dolphins

Moreton Bay is home to approximately 600 bottlenose dolphins and, just on sunset, Tangalooma is visited by a small pod which frequent the shores to feed, hunt and play. You are encouraged to learn and identify these endearing creatures by their individual and quite distinctive dorsal fin markings. Anyone can join on the jetty to watch this nightly spectacle; however, if you wish to join in the hand-feeding you must be an overnight guest at the resort or be booked on the resort's extended day tour with dolphin-feeding. You will also need to register at the resort's Marine Education and Conservation Centre from 1–5pm.

Food and Drink

❶ BEACH CAFÉ

Tangalooma Island Resort; tel: 3410 6000; www.tangalooma.com; Mon–Fri 11.30am–2.30pm, Sat–Sun 11.30am–9pm; $$
This ultra-casual beachside café offers pizzas, pastas, burgers, salads and a delicious cold seafood platter, as well as children's meals.

❷ TURSIOPS BUFFET RESTAURANT

Tangalooma Island Resort; tel: 3410 6000; www.tangalooma.com; daily 6–9pm in season (check prior to visit); $$$
Casual buffet fare is offered at this spot, which prides itself on a monster breakfast, but also offers lunch daily and dinner on Saturdays.

Enjoying Noosa Main Beach

SUNSHINE COAST

Discover natural beauty and charming settlements by leaving the highway to pass through the eerie Glass House Mountains and remnant rainforests on the way to the ridge-top villages of Maleny and Montville, before descending to the chic beachside resort of Noosa.

DISTANCE: 170km (102 miles)
TIME: A full day
START: Brisbane
END: Noosa National Park
POINTS TO NOTE: You will need a car for this full-day adventure. If you start by 8am, you will be able to fit everything in with plenty of stops, but there is so much to see and so much worth doing on the Sunshine Coast that, if time permits, stretching this route out into a two- or even three-day excursion. If you time your trip so you pass through Eumundi on a Wednesday or Saturday, try to catch the popular Eumundi Markets.

The Sunshine Coast is a glorious stretch of coastline extending about 120km (72 miles) from Bribie Island in the south to Rainbow Beach, near Fraser Island, in the north. Compared to the Gold Coast, commercial development is more restrained; though there are still high-rise towers and shopping malls, you are never too far away from a peaceful expanse of golden beach. Noosa is the jewel in the coastal crown, an unlikely encapsulation of luxury, hedonism and natural beauty that rarely fails to charm visitors. Back from the beach, the rolling green hills of the hinterland are peppered with gorgeous villages and mysterious volcanic mountains.

GLASS HOUSE MOUNTAINS

Head north from Brisbane on the Bruce Highway for approximately 56km (34 miles) and turn left at The Glasshouse Mountains Tourist Drive, also known as the Steve Irwin Way since the death of 'The Crocodile Hunter'. This is where you will catch your first really good glimpses of the **Glass House Mountains ❶**. These unusual volcanic plugs are the remains of lava-belching volcanoes that violently issued from the earth some 20 million years ago. The craggy, eroded peaks in the eponymous national park (see www.nprsr.gov.au) offer impressive walking tracks to panoramic lookouts, while the well-drained slopes of rich volcanic soil around the mountains are ideal for growing pineapples, which are

The atmospheric Glass House Mountains

sold by the bucket load at roadside stalls, along with avocados, macadamia nuts and other produce.

AUSTRALIA ZOO

About 2km (1.25 miles) past Beerwah, a sign directs you to **Australia Zoo ②** (Steve Irwin Way, Beerwah; www.australia zoo.com.au; daily 9am–5pm; charge). This started out as a small reptile park in the 1970s, created by Bob and Lyn Irwin, but thanks to his irrepressible character and antics with dangerous critters, most notably crocodiles, their son, Steve 'The Crocodile Hunter' Irwin, turned it into a world-renowned zoo. Steve was killed by a stingray in 2006, but his legacy of hands-on conservation continues at the zoo. Living within natural Australian and recreated Asian habitats are numerous mammals, birds and reptiles, and there are a number of daily shows. Bus tours from Brisbane and the Sunshine Coast are also available if you want to come back.

Boomerangs at Eumundi Markets

At Landsborough, turn left and drive up the hill, following the signs and the winding road towards Maleny. As you climb, remember to check out the splendid views of patchwork farms and the coast far to the east. There are many designated spots to stop the car, whip out the camera and capture the countryside, so take advantage of them.

MARY CAIRNCROSS SCENIC RESERVE

After 9km (5.5 miles), turn left at Cairncross Corner off the main Maleny road, to **Mary Cairncross Scenic Reserve** ❸ (www.mary-cairncross.com.au). The reserve protects a remnant of the magnificent subtropical rainforest that once covered these ranges. There are easy trails (including some that are wheelchair-accessible) through the rainforest, offering unobstructed views of the cultivated valleys, rugged Glass House Mountains and distant coastline. For a late breakfast or early lunch, head to the delightful **Café**, see ❶.

MALENY

Continue on the same road for 9km (5.5 miles), following the signposted tourist drive, which loops north to the hill township of **Maleny** ❹ – a picturesque country town with beautiful colonial architecture occupied by new-age shops, galleries and craft outlets. Many talented artists and craftspeople have made this their home, and you may just find that something special here that is genuinely Australian and original.

MONTVILLE

Head east on the Maleny–Landsborough Road for 4km (2.5 miles) before taking a left turn to Montville, which lies around 10km (6 miles) further north. Again you will enjoy spectacular ridgetop vistas en route, plus a few glimpses of scenic Lake Baroon. **Montville** ❺, visually even more of a chocolate-box town than Maleny, is ornamented with determinedly quaint shops offering all manner of arts and crafts. The main street is well worth a wander, with numerous options for eating and drinking, such as **The Edge Restaurant**, see ❷.

EUMUNDI

Head east again for a further 15km (9 miles) to the Bruce Highway, and then turn left towards Nambour to reach Eumundi after 26km (16 miles). Yet another charming hinterland town, **Eumundi** ❻ is decorated with contemporary artwork by local artists; mingling with the historic buildings are shops selling new-age paraphernalia and jewellery, along with plenty of cafés. But it is the renowned markets (Memorial Drive, Eumundi; Wed 8am–1.30pm and Sat 6.30am–2pm) that have put Eumundi on the map. Some 20,000 people – both locals and visitors – flock here twice a

A koala at Australia Zoo

Surfers at Noosa Main Beach

week to peruse hundreds of stalls selling local produce, arts and crafts, crystals and much more. From Eumundi, it is 21km (13 miles) northeast via Route 12 to the coast at Noosa.

NOOSA

You wouldn't be the first to ask, what is Noosa? The area includes Noosaville, set back on the Noosa River; Noosa Junction; and Sunshine Beach, but for most people the name really refers to the compact area called **Noosa Heads ❼**.

Located on the sandy shore of Laguna Bay at the mouth of the river and overlooked by a rugged natural headland, the main Noosa 'strip' is **Hastings Street**, where the chintziest shops, finest restaurants and beautiful people all come together to epitomise the Noosa fairytale. All your information and booking needs are met by the **Noosa Visitor Centre** (Hastings Street; www.visit noosa.com.au; daily 9am–5pm). Directly in front of Hastings Street is **Noosa Main Beach**, where you can try surfing or just enjoy the golden sand and gentle waves.

Around Noosa Heads
Other places to explore locally include **Noosa National Park ❽** south of town, and **Noosa North Shore**, across the river. The **Queensland Parks and Wildlife Service Information Centre** (daily 9am–3pm) in Noosa National Park is just a few minutes' walk from Hastings Street, and from there you can access walking trails where you might spot koalas and admire spectacular views of the Pacific Ocean and Sunshine Coast. Noosa North Shore is the start of the remote **Cooloola Coast** (www.cooloola.org.au), which stretches right up to **Rainbow Beach**. It is accessed by a ferry near Tewantin and is best explored by 4WD, but even without a 4WD, activities such as horse and camel riding can be organised; ask for more details at the Noosa Visitor Centre.

Food and Drink

❶ CAFÉ AT MARY CAIRNCROSS SCENIC RESERVE
148 Mountain View Road, Maleny; tel: 5494 2287; www.mary-cairncross.com. au; Tue–Sun 8.30am–4.30pm, until 4pm in winter; $
Breakfast on organic muesli or eggs and bacon (at least until 11.30am) or lunch on variations of BLTs, burgers and salads. The coffee is organic and fairtrade, as befits the natural setting.

❷ THE EDGE RESTAURANT
The Mayfield Centre, 127–133 Main Street, Montville; tel: 5442 9344; 9am–4pm; $$
If you can take your eyes off the spectacular hinterland views that stretch away to the Pacific Ocean, you will find a light and seasonal Modern Australian menu of pasta dishes, salads, steaks and seafood here, in dishes such as salt-and-pepper prawns.

NORTH STRADBROKE ISLAND

North Stradbroke has long been Brisbane's favourite escape. Seemingly endless white-sand beaches, freshwater lagoons and wilderness walks will delight back-to-nature types, and for those who'd prefer not to go 'bush', there are also plenty of options for pampered relaxation and fine dining.

DISTANCE: 71km (43 miles), not including drive on Main Beach
TIME: A full day
START/END: Dunwich
POINTS TO NOTE: A 4WD is needed for the full route to be explored, although a conventional car is fine if you plan on leaving out the beach driving. Vehicle ferries and water taxis access the island from Cleveland Ferry Terminal, 35km (21 miles) southeast of Brisbane CBD; to catch a 9am ferry, be sure to leave Brisbane by 7.45am. The ferry crossing takes 45 minutes. Ferry operators include Big Red Cat (www.big redcat.com.au) and Stradbroke Ferries (www.stradbrokeferries.com.au). You must book in advance, and the ferry company can arrange your beach access (driving) permit. Along with the permit, you will get a tide chart.

North Stradbroke, or 'Straddie' to the locals, is an island of immense natural beauty and, at 38km (23 miles) long and 11km (7 miles) wide, it is the world's second-largest sand island, after Fraser Island (see page 63). It has been home to the Nunukul, Nughie and Goenpul peoples, who know it as Minjerribah, for many thousands of years – artefacts and evidence of Aboriginal settlement date back over 20,000 years. European settlement stretches back a more modest 185 years, to a time when a shipping pilot station was established at Amity Point. Today's small permanent population of approximately 3,000 swells considerably at weekends and during public holidays.

DUNWICH

The small fishing township of **Dunwich** ❶ was used variously by the Europeans as a convict outstation, a Catholic mission, a quarantine station and a benevolent institution. A Heritage Trail leads walkers around the many buildings remaining from this period and winds through convict relics and graves dating right back to those shipwrecked in the 1800s. Pick up details from the **Strad-**

Cylinder Beach

broke Island Tourist Information Centre (Junner Street; www.stradbroke tourism.com; daily 8.30am–4.30pm).

The **North Stradbroke Island Historical Museum** (15–17 Welsby Street; www.stradbrokemuseum.com; Tue–Sat 10am–2pm, Sun 11am–3pm; charge), housed in an original dormitory of the benevolent institution, offers an impressive display of photographs and items retrieved from shipwrecks, as well as information about Aboriginal and pioneer settlements, and the sand-mining industry.

POINT LOOKOUT

From Dunwich, drive 19km (12 miles) northeast to the township of **Point Lookout ❷**. Named by James Cook in 1770, this is Queensland's most easterly point and is one of the best land-based vantage points to witness the acrobatic antics of magnificent humpback whales. Flipper-slapping, tail-waving and mighty breaching leaps that result in explosive splashdowns can all be witnessed as the whales pass by here from June to November, on their annual migration

Taking a canoe to the beach

north. All summer they will have been feeding in the rich waters of Antarctica, and now they are heading for their calmer calving grounds in the Coral Sea.

The rocky headland shelters several excellent beaches, such as Deadman's (unpatrolled but good for exploring rock pools), Cylinder (a patrolled surf beach, ideal for families), Home (unpatrolled) and Flinders (unpatrolled, 4WDs allowed).

Do what Cook certainly did not do and enjoy a refreshing morning tea break at the **Oceanic Gelati & Coffee Bar**, see ❶, and then cross the road to start the spectacular **North Gorge Walk** (the path begins beside the public toilet block). It's only a little over 1km (0.65 mile) and the views are superb. As the pathway clings to the edge of the coast, keep your eyes on the water and watch out for humpback whales. Often it's possible to spot large pods of dolphins, graceful manta rays, sharks and turtles, all swimming freely in the sparkling blue waters below. In places you can walk out onto the rocky coastline to sit and watch the marine wildlife show and admire the powerful waves crashing into the shore. Further along, the walk ventures onto **South Gorge** and then the sweeping expanse of Main Beach comes into view. As the path ends and heads towards the road, turn right and you will discover that you are only a short distance away from your starting point.

The views from Point Lookout are truly sublime, and to continue the expe-rience over lunch, drive back along the road you came in on to the **Stradbroke Island Beach Hotel & Spa Resort**, see ❷, known to locals simply as the Straddie Pub. In whale-watching season you can sit and eat your fresh fish and chips here while watching whales breach and splash below.

MAIN BEACH

Just to the west of the Straddie Pub there is a turnoff to the south onto George Nothling Drive, with signposts indicating access to **Main Beach** ❸. (Before heading down this way, consult your tide chart, as beach driving is best an hour or so either side of low tide and is prohibited an hour either side of high tide.) This amazing stretch of pristine white beach is legendary with Stradbroke regulars. Surfers rise to the challenge on these waves, fishermen cast into the deep 'gutters' (channels between the breaks), pulling in dinner, and you can easily find a patch of lonely beach to comb.

At the right time, it is possible to drive the entire 34km (21-mile) length of beach to **Jumpinpin**, the sea channel between North and South Stradbroke islands. The two islands were once connected.

AMITY POINT

It is a 12km (7.5 mile) drive west from Point Lookout to **Amity** ❹, a down-to-earth fishing village on the island's northwestern tip. A pilot station was

Prawn trawlers · *On Amity's jetty at sunset*

established here in 1825 and Amity became the main access point for boats coming from Brisbane over the next 150 years. These days, families come here for the beachside camping, calm waters, good fishing and safe swimming (although, it's worth noting, Amity Point was the scene of a fatal shark attack in 2006, with the victim taken in waist-deep water).

BROWN AND BLUE LAKES

From Amity Point, retrace your drive back out onto the East Coast Road and turn right for Dunwich. If you have time to spare before your return ferry, **Brown Lake** ❺ is only 4km (2.5 miles) east of Dunwich, and it is worth taking a glimpse at this perched lake, part of the island's amazing freshwater lake system. The water is stained tea-brown by the surrounding trees, reeds and organic matter, but you can take a refreshing swim in its cool embrace, or wander the walking trail around its shore. Alternatively, **Blue Lake** ❻ is 10km (6 miles) east of Dunwich (accessible by a conventional car), and from the car park it is a further 3km (1.65-mile) walk (approximately 30 minutes). The gin-like water laps clean white sand, turning a rich blue colour as the lake deepens. Wildlife abounds, especially in the early morning or late afternoon, and it's common to spot swamp wallabies and sand goannas.

Head back to Dunwich to catch the ferry back to Brisbane, and if there is time for an afternoon tea stop, visit the **Island Fruit Barn**, see ❸, in town.

Food and Drink

❶ OCEANIC GELATI & COFFEE BAR

19 Mooloomba Road, Point Lookout; tel: 3415 3222; daily 9.30am–5pm; $

Choose from a great range of fruit juices, smoothies, gelato and coffee. Especially good is the affogato – espresso poured over ice cream.

❷ STRADBROKE ISLAND BEACH HOTEL & SPA RESORT

East Coast Road, Point Lookout; tel: 3409 8188; www.stradbrokehotel.com.au; daily 7.30–10am, 11.30am–2.30pm, 5.30–8.30pm; $$$

Overlooking the beach, the bistro and beer garden of the 'Straddie Pub' offer an excellent choice of local seafood, including Straddie prawns and beer-battered coral trout, plus succulent steaks, pizzas, and meals for little 'nippers'.

❸ ISLAND FRUIT BARN

16 Bingle Road, Dunwich; tel: 3409 9125; Mon–Fri 7am–5pm, Sat–Sun 7am–4pm; $$

This atypical fruit barn adds value to its array of seasonal fruits and vegetables by tempting travellers with fresh salads, organic fruit smoothies, delicious cakes and decent coffee.

Apartment buildings in Surfers Paradise

GOLD COAST

Queensland's Gold Coast is not just a surfer's paradise. On this driving route you can certainly catch waves, but also explore the region's golden shores and glittering malls, take to its high-rise towers, and discover its quiet corners and natural charm.

DISTANCE: 102km (61 miles)
TIME: A full day
START: Brisbane
END: Currumbin Wildlife Sanctuary
POINTS TO NOTE: Don't forget your swimming gear, hat and sunscreen. If time permits, extend your stay to fully enjoy the theme parks, surf and plethora of natural and man-made attractions this area offers. You can also combine this route with Route 7. The Gold Coast is easily accessed by bus or train-and-bus combination from Brisbane, and there are bus connections directly from Brisbane Airport. The Gold Coast also has its own airport at Coolangatta, 25km (15.5 miles) south of Surfers Paradise.

The post-war boom of the late 1940s saw this area wake to a future full of potential, and opportunists have continued to make it their home. The hedonistic lifestyle and garishness that characterises the high-rise section of The Strip culminates in Surfers Paradise, Queensland's answer to Miami or Ipanema. However, the Gold Coast is not only a stretch of golden beaches with a backdrop of skyscrapers, a concentration of colourful theme parks and a culture of conspicuous commercialism. As you move along the coast away from 'Paradise', you'll discover more natural beauty. The surf beaches, particularly Burleigh Heads set in national parkland, are strikingly gorgeous.

MAIN BEACH

From Brisbane, drive southeast for 64km (40 miles) on the Southeast Freeway (Route 3), which becomes the Pacific Motorway (M1). You will pass signs to several theme parks (see page 24), as most are concentrated at the northwestern end of the coastal strip, just off the motorway. At Helensvale, turn off at Exit 62 onto the Gold Coast Highway and drive for 13km (8 miles) to **Main Beach ❶**. This has long been a favoured spot for the stylish and wealthy, and those who enjoy chic boutiques and being seen in trendy cafés.

The view from Skypoint   *Soaking up the sun on Main Beach*

The Spit is a 3km (2-mile) sandbar running north of Main Beach, separating the Broadwater from the Coral Sea. Head along Seaworld Drive where, on the left you will find the **Marina Mirage** (www.marinamirage.com.au; daily 10am–6pm), a luxury boat marina combined with an upmarket shopping complex of fashion boutiques, cafés and restaurants. Indulge in chocolate for morning tea at **Max Brenner Chocolate Bar**, see ❶, drop in to admire the opulence of the **Palazzo Versace Hotel** next door, or window-shop the classy boutiques.

Also adjacent to Marina Mirage is **Mariners Cove (Fisherman's Wharf)**, with yet more dining options as well as numerous companies offering watersport activities from fishing to jet boating. Further along the Spit is **Sea World**.

SURFER'S PARADISE

Continue south on the Gold Coast Highway for 3km (2 miles) to **Surfers Paradise** ❷, the flashy pendant on this stretch of coastline bling. Epitomising the quirky and superficial culture of Surfers is the continued presence of the strip's famous Meter Maids. First introduced in 1965 to put a positive spin on the fact that parking meters had been installed on the tourist

Bright lights at night from Skypoint

strip, the maids are young women clad in tiaras and gold bikinis, who walk the streets putting coins into meters.

But it was the surf that first lured people to these beaches, and it's the surf that provides the prime attraction, so factor in some time to enjoy it.

When you're done with swimming, surfing or just lying about, check out **Skypoint** (Q1 Surfers Paradise Boulevard; www.skypoint.com.au, Sun–Thur 9am–9pm, Fri–Sat 9am–midnight; charge), one of the Gold Coast's essential attractions. Here you will ascend to Level 77 of the world's tallest residential building, rising 322m (1,056ft) into the sky for breathtaking 360-degree views that extend up and down the coast from Brisbane to Byron Bay.

For lunch beside the ocean with a dose of Aussie beach culture, walk a few blocks south along the shoreline to the **Northcliffe Surf Lifesaving Club**, see ➋.

BROADBEACH

A short 2km (1.25 miles) hop south is **Broadbeach** ➌, a slightly less frenetic and more family friendly town than Surfers, but still a zone of residential towers, shopping malls and tempting eateries. For some retail therapy, turn right into Hooker Boulevard and stop at the enormous **Pacific Fair Shopping Centre** (www.pacificfair.com.au; Fri–Sat 9am–5.30pm, Thur until 9pm, Sun 10am–4pm), which is jam-packed with fashion stores. Across the road is **Conrad Jupiters Casino** (www.jupiterscasino.com.au; daily 24 hours). With seven restaurants and five bars, plus the gaming tables and machines, there's no end to the ways you can lighten your wallet here.

BURLEIGH HEADS

A further 8km (5 miles) south brings you to **Burleigh Heads** ➍, the Gold Coast's premier family destination. Here the beaches are backed by beautiful parkland, and you can sit on the grass under beachside pines and palms while watching the surfers take on some of Austral-

---

Learn to surf

The Gold Coast is one of the great surfing meccas of the world, with excellent beach breaks all along the coast, so it makes sense to grab both a board and an instructor to give the sport a try. Beginner lessons are generally two hours long, and start with honing your technique on the sand before heading to the water for the exhilaration of standing up on your board for the first time. Several surf schools are located up and down the coast. At the Cheyne Horan School of Surf (The Esplanade, Surfers Paradise; www.cheynehoran.com.au), the former world surfing champion and his small team of instructors offer daily beginner classes at 10am and 2pm, as well as complimentary hotel pick-up anywhere from Broadbeach to Southport.

Currumbin Wildlife

Surfers Paradise is a modern beach town

ia's best waves. A block back from the beach, have yourself a big feed at **The Little Plate**, see ❸.

Burleigh Head National Park (veer left along Goodwin Terrace as you come into Burleigh Heads) is fantastic for views. If you're keen to stretch your legs, the 2.5km (1.5-mile) **Ocean View Circuit** leads around the rocky headland from Tallebudgera Creek to the southern edge of Burleigh Heads Township.

CURRUMBIN WILDLIFE SANCTUARY

Six kilometres (4 miles) south of Burleigh Heads is one of the Gold Coast's oldest tourist attractions, **Currumbin Wildlife Sanctuary** ❺ (28 Tomewin Street, Currumbin; www.cws.org.au; daily 8am–5pm; charge), which continues to delight kids of all ages with interactive wildlife displays. At the time of writing, the sanctuary had ceased its nocturnal tours, but look out for their new evening initiatives in the future.

From Currumbin you can head back to Brisbane, about 100km (63 miles) away on the Pacific Motorway, or find accommodation on the Gold Coast (see page 103) and continue the tour of the Gold Coast Hinterland (see page 60).

Food and Drink

❶ MAX BRENNER CHOCOLATE BAR

Ground Floor, Marina Mirage, 74 Seaworld Drive, Main Beach; tel: 5591 1588; www.maxbrenner.com.au; Mon–Thur 10am–10pm, Fri 10am–midnight, Sat 9am–midnight, Sun 9am–10pm; $$
If you can't resist the smells wafting from the doorway, sit down surrounded by everything chocolate to drink or munch on. Coffee is also available.

❷ NORTHCLIFFE SURF LIFESAVING CLUB BISTRO

At Garfield Terrace and Thornton Street, Surfers Paradise; tel: 5539 8091; www.bmdnorthcliffe.com.au; daily 7.30am–9pm; $$

Beachside surf lifesaving clubs are iconic in Australia, and at this one you can watch the action on the beach while enjoying a casual and extensive menu that includes everything from burgers, baguettes, sandwiches, pasta and pizza to chargrilled meats and seafood dishes.

❸ THE LITTLE PLATE

11/3 Deodar drive, Burleigh Heads; tel: 0499 724 30; Breakfast, lunch and late; $$
With a relaxed attitude to everything from shared plates to opening hours, this informal and friendly little restaurant is serious only about one thing: the quality of its food, which is served from a brilliantly varied menu offering tasty titbits from right around the world cuisine. Hard to go past the local seafood, though, the squid is sublime.

Walking in Lamington National Park

GOLD COAST HINTERLAND

Behind the cement-and-glass forests of the Gold Coast is a verdant hinterland of rugged ranges sheltering villages, plunging waterfalls and nature retreats. Much of this stunning landscape is protected in three National Parks: Tamborine, Lamington and Springbrook.

DISTANCE: 170km (102 miles)
TIME: Two days
START: Oxenford turnoff
END: Springbrook National Park
POINTS TO NOTE: This is a driving route. From Brisbane, head southeast for about 60km (36 miles) on the Southeast Freeway (Route 3), which becomes the Pacific Motorway (M1), exiting at Oxenford. If you are starting this route from the Gold Coast, either head north along the Gold Coast Highway and the Pacific Motorway to exit at Oxenford, or access the Pacific Motorway at Nerang. From the Oxenford exit off the motorway, head west for about 2km (1.25 miles) before turning right onto the Tamborine–Oxenford Road and following a 19km (11.5-mile) route that takes you to Eagle Heights.

About an hour's drive from either Brisbane or the Gold Coast high-rises is a realm of lush rainforests, waterfalls and glorious natural vistas. The bush that forms the Gold Coast's green backdrop is in stark contrast to the hype of the coastal strip and is the ideal hangover cure after sampling the party lifestyle. The rugged ranges that challenged the pioneers and cedar-getters now embrace spas, wineries, cheese factories and craft stalls. There are also several 'islands' of native bush protected in National Parks offering idyllic nature-focused retreats.

MOUNT TAMBORINE

The winding road from the **Oxenford turnoff** on the Pacific Motorway ascends for 19km (11.5 miles) through a mixture of native bush and rolling pastures to Eagle Heights with sweeping views of the Gold Coast, its hinterland and the ocean beyond. This mountain oasis comprises the three close-knit heritage communities of Mount Tamborine, North Tamborine and Eagle Heights, and is collectively referred to as **Mount Tamborine**. The **Visitor Information Centre** (Doughty Park, Main Western Road, North Tamborine; www.tamborinemt-ncc.org.au; daily 10am–4pm) can pro-

Panoramic view   *Rapids in Lamington National Park*

vide maps of the local roads, bushwalks and National Parks.

Eagle Heights

Gallery Walk in **Eagle Heights ❶** is the mountain community's shopping precinct and is filled with an array of touristy craft shops, galleries and alfresco eateries. For morning tea, head to **Granny Macs Store**, see ❶. Continue to the end

of Gallery Walk (it turns into Long Road) and turn left into Curtis Road. At the end of this road there is access to a beautiful 900m/yd rainforest walk to **Cedar Creek Falls**, part of **Tamborine National Park ❷**. If you are extending your stay there are many other great walks in this National Park that comprises 14 separate parcels of land, one of which, **Witches Falls**, was Queensland's first National Park. Well worth a detour while you're here is Australia's smallest operating pot distillery, **Tamborine Mountain Distillery** (87–91 Beacon Road, North Tamborine; www.tamborinemountain distillery.com; Mon–Sat 10am–3pm), which has won international awards for its liqueurs, schnapps, vodkas and fruit brandies, flavoured by the amazing range and quality of fruit grown on Mount Tamborine's rich volcanic soils. There's a delightful organic farm and distillery, and they do cellar-door sales.

LAMINGTON NATIONAL PARK

From North Tamborine take the Tamborine Mountain Road south to Mount Tamborine and continue towards Canungra, turning left at the Canungra–Nerang crossroads and right a little further on at the Beechmont/Binna Burra road. You have now descended into the **Coomera River Valley** and are climbing the opposite ridge to the hilltop village of Beechmont. Turn right here for the 10km (6-mile) drive to **Binna Burra Mountain Lodge** (see page 104), 800m (2,600ft)

Natural Bridge, at Springbrook National Park

above sea level, in the World Heritage–listed 20,000ha (50,000-acre) **Lamington National Park ❸**. The lodge was the first resort in the region to gain official ecotourism accreditation.

Detailed walking maps and park brochures are available at the **National Parks and Wildlife Information Centre** (tel: 5533 3584; Mon–Fri 7.30am–4pm, Sat and Sun 9am–3pm), just before the Lodge. The **Rainforest Circuit** is an easy 30-minute walk, while the short **Bellbird Lookout Walk** offers excellent views of towering rocky bluffs and the Numinbah Valley. The valley used to be the forest habitat of the valuable hoop pine and the red cedar, the harvesting of which led to the establishment of the first European settlement here, which in turn ultimately resulted in the clearing of the valley.

SPRINGBROOK NATIONAL PARK

Return down the same route via Beechmont, but turn right close to the bottom of the hill and take the Nerang–Murwillumbah road (Route 97) via Advancetown. This takes you up the scenic **Numinbah Valley to the Natural Bridge** (also known as the Natural Arch) section of **Springbrook National Park ❹**. About 25km (15 miles) from the Advancetown turn-off, you will find the Natural Bridge car park. A 1km (0.65-mile) circular walk brings you to this peculiar formation where **Cave Creek** stream plunges through the eroded roof of an underground basalt cavern; you can enter further down the

pathway to view the waterfall. For more waterfalls, make the detour to take the 4km (2.5-mile) **Purlingbrook Falls** circuit walk through the Springbrook Plateau section of the national park, which has excellent bushwalks and stunning waterfalls. Allow two to three hours to do the circuit walk, which starts from the Gwongorella picnic area. To get there, return down the Nerang–Murwillumbah road and, after 11km (6.5 miles), turn right and right again onto the Springbrook Road (Route 99). The Dancing Waters Cafe next to the car park is a good bet for a snack or a light lunch. Additionally, the Best of All Lookout lives up to its name.

From Natural Bridge it is 100km (60 miles) to Brisbane. Head back down the Nerang–Murwillumbah Road, continue straight on the Beaudesert–Nerang Road, following signs to Nerang. At Nerang you will merge onto the Pacific Motorway for the 71km (42.5-mile) trip back to Brisbane.

Food and Drink

❶ GRANNY MACS STORE

139 Gallery Walk, Eagle Heights; tel: 5545 1999; www.grannymacs.com; daily 9am–5pm; $

Relax on the veranda and enjoy Devonshire tea, pancakes, or a light meal such as soup or salad. The store is also renowned for its wide variety of fudge – all made on the premises.

Kingfisher Bay Resort

GOLD COAST HINTERLAND

This three-day 4WD adventure takes you through an extraordinary wilderness where flourishing rainforests, pristine freshwater lakes and streams, and desert-like sand dunes are accessed via long, lonely highways of sand. This is the world's largest sand island and an area of rare beauty.

DISTANCE: 157km (94 miles), mostly on day two
TIME: Three days
START/END: Kingfisher Bay
POINTS TO NOTE: For the 12.30pm ferry to the island from River Heads, 300km (186 miles) north of Brisbane, pre-book a ticket (www.fraserislandferry.com.au) and leave the city by 7am. Take the Bruce Highway to the Maryborough exit and follow signs to Hervey Bay and River Heads. Collect your ticket at least 20 minutes prior to departure. You can also fly to Hervey Bay. River Heads has a café and store to buy picnic supplies for lunch. Hire a 4WD vehicle in Brisbane, Hervey Bay or at Kingfisher Bay Resort. A beach-driving permit must be obtained, either from Queensland Parks and Wildlife Service (http://parks.nprsr.qld.gov.au) or from the ferry before you board.

Fraser Island was listed as a UNESCO World Heritage Area in 1992, an act that recognised its significant natural features, including dune, lake and forest ecosystems. A great variety of plant species on the island grow entirely on sand and range from coastal heath to mangrove forests, swamps and subtropical rainforests.

Evidence suggests that the indigenous Butchulla people (now living on the mainland) occupied these parts for more than 5,500 years. Their name for the island was K'gari, which fittingly means paradise. Although logging and sand mining become major industries after European discovery, they were halted a couple of decades ago, allowing Fraser Island to recover its natural state.

One of Fraser Island's biggest attractions are its dingoes, which remain very pure. As hunters and scavengers, however, they are wild and unpredictable, and have been known to attack humans, so keep all food secure and do not leave rubbish or scraps lying around.

KINGFISHER BAY RESORT

From River Heads on the mainland, it takes 50 minutes to reach **Kingfisher Bay Resort ❶**. This, the larger of the

4WD tours of Fraser Island are very popular

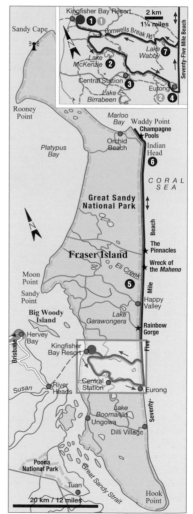

island's two resorts, nestles on the edge of the Great Sandy Strait on Fraser Island's western shore. It is a multi-award-winning ecotourism resort with accommodation designed to conserve energy, minimise waste and blend with the surrounding bush.

LAKE MCKENZIE

On the first afternoon, take to the island's inland bush tracks, following signs from the resort, to drive 12km (7 miles) southeast to Lake McKenzie. From now on you will be driving on sand tracks, generally only wide enough for one vehicle, so it is important to be vigilant for oncoming 4WDs. The drive time will depend on the condition of the track: if conditions are dry and rough, vehicles may become bogged and cause delays to your journey. A good run from Kingfisher Bay to Lake McKenzie will take 45 minutes, but it could take double that. Remember to pack water and food, as there are no facilities en route.

At the end of your winding drive through lush vegetation, **Lake McKenzie** ❷ will dazzle you with its translucent blue water, washing above pure white sand. Sitting 100m (330ft) above sea level and covering more than 150ha (370 acres), this perched lake is not fed by streams or groundwater but contains only rainwater filtered by the sand, making the water so pure it can support very little life.

Take the time to swim and laze on the soft sandy shores, before returning

Wanggoolba Creek

Rusty remnants of the Maheno

to Kingfisher Resort for sunset cocktails out on the jetty, or a stroll along the beach before a buffet-style dinner where the focus is on locally sourced ingredients at **Maheno Restaurant**, see ❶.

CENTRAL STATION

The order in which you do things on the second day will be determined by tide times. The best beach driving will be at low tide or within two hours either side. The following itinerary has been based on low tide happening in the middle of the day.

After breakfast, depart by 8am for the 14km (8.5-mile) drive southeast to Central Station. From the resort, take the first sign that says Lake McKenzie. At the next junction, take a right turn onto Bennett Road, follow for approximately 6km (3.5 miles), then turn left at the next junction.

Originally an old logging depot, **Central Station** ❸ crouches under towering bunya pines and is now the starting point for many pretty walks into the surrounding areas. The **Pile Valley Circuit Walk** is a 4.5km (3-mile) boardwalk around **Wanggoolba Creek**, an astonishingly clear and pristine stream. The walk then winds through awesome satinay trees that grow to more than 60m (197ft).

Return to your vehicle and continue 8km (5 miles) east, following the signs to Eurong Beach Resort.

SEVENTY-FIVE MILE BEACH

The small village of **Eurong** ❹ has a resort and limited facilities, but you can buy petrol and a small selection of groceries. There is one restaurant, McKenzie's **Restaurant**, see ❷, and a bakery, which is a good place to buy a picnic lunch.

From Eurong Beach Resort, continue your journey out onto **Seventy-Five Mile Beach**, to head 30km (19 miles) north to Eli Creek.

As the name suggests, **Seventy-Five Mile Beach** is a 120km (75-mile) stretch of uninterrupted sand, also known as the Eastern Beach, running up the eastern side of the island and flanked by dunes and rolling ocean. While driving, be alert to ocean surges, soft sand, and freshwater springs that run out from the dunes to the ocean, sometimes causing small washouts. Standard road rules apply when driving on the beach, including keeping to the left of oncoming vehicles. Small aircraft also use Seventy-Five Mile Beach as a landing strip. Aeroplanes need to land on the harder sand found close to the water's edge, so vehicles should move to the upper beach nearer the high tide line.

Millions of litres of fresh water pour out of **Eli Creek** ❺ every hour, and visitors love to swim and float down the clear-flowing stream. For an elevated view of the creek, walk the 400m/yd **Eli Creek Boardwalk**; it takes about 15 minutes.

On Indian Head boardwalk

Keep driving for 5km (3 miles) to reach the relic of the **Maheno**, a passenger liner that ran aground in 1935.

Indian Head

From the *Maheno*, continue 25km (15 miles) north along the beach to Indian Head. On the way, look for the colourful sand cliffs near the stretch called Cathedral Beach. One section, **The Pinnacles**, has a stunning display of yellows, browns, reds and oranges, sculpted by nature. On arrival at **Indian Head** ❻, climb to the top of this headland and you might spot whales, sharks, rays, turtles and schools of fish in the waters below.

From Indian Head it is a 3km (2-mile) drive north to the **Champagne Pools**. These saltwater rockpools are especially beautiful at low tide, while at high tide waves crash over the rocks creating 'champagne bubbles'.

RETURN JOURNEY

The return journey back down the beach to Eurong is 63km (38 miles), but look out for a more direct sand track approximately 6km (3.5 miles) before you get to Eurong. Known as Cornwells Break Road, you can follow it from Seventy-Five Mile Beach for 15km (9 miles) back to **Kingfisher Bay Resort**. Grab dinner in the signature **Seabelle Restaurant** (see page 116).

LAKE WABBY

Lake Wabby ❼ is another of the island's stunning lakes, perfect for a morning swim. Set out early and turn left onto the Cornwells Break Road. After 13km (8 miles), turn right for Lake Wabby (the drive takes at least an hour). Park the car and walk the 15-minute trail to the lake, where you will be met by the shifting sands of **Stonetool Sand Blow** and the emerald waters of Lake Wabby. Leave enough time for your return journey to Kingfisher Bay Resort, and catch the 2pm reutrn ferry to River Heads to make it back to Brisbane by early evening.

Food and Drink

❶ MAHENO RESTAURANT

Kingfisher Bay Resort, Fraser Island; tel: 4120 3333; www.kingfisherbay.com; daily 6.30am–10pm; $$–$$$

Maheno operates with a 'Paddock to Plate' approach, which means where possible the produce is sourced locally. Dinner is buffet-style, offering a selection of hot and cold dishes including local fish, king prawns and their renowned mornay of Hervey Bay scallops.

❷ MCKENZIE'S RESTAURANT

Eurong Beach Resort; tel: 4120 1600; www.eurong.com; daily 6.30am–8pm; $$

This casual restaurant with attached bar serves a buffet lunch (11.30am–2pm) of soup, salad and hot dishes, and overlooks an inviting free-form swimming pool.

White sands and crystal-clear waters

WHITSUNDAY ISLANDS

On this five-day camping and kayaking route you have the opportunity to connect with the 'other' Whitsundays. Away from the tourist crowds and pampering resorts, you will be following Aboriginal migration routes, sleeping under the stars and exploring lonely beaches on a self-propelled paddling adventure.

DISTANCE: Varies
TIME: Five days
START/END: Airlie Beach
POINTS TO NOTE: Airlie Beach, gateway to the Whitsundays, is served by the long-distance buses that ply the East Coast. You can also fly straight into the islands via Hamilton Island Airport, which has regular flights to/from both Cairns and Brisbane. Tents and cooking utensils can be hired and drinking water and food bought at Airlie Beach. A reasonable level of fitness is required for this route, along with sturdy footwear, hat, sunscreen and insect repellent. The ideal months for camping are from May to December.

The Whitsunday Islands form one of the world's most scenic adventure playgrounds. Hundreds of secluded bays, coves and deserted beaches are dotted throughout this calm corner of the Coral Sea, which is sheltered by the Great Barrier Reef. For thousands of years, the Ngaro people lived throughout this area, leaving behind rock art, fish traps, stone tools and middens. By following part of the Ngaro Sea Trail, you will paddle in their wake while experiencing the region's natural splendour.

This is not the usual way to experience the Whitsundays; you will not be visiting lavish resorts or cruising in luxury vessels. You will be self-sufficient, but your rewards will be lonely white-sand beaches, encounters with ancient rock art and deliciously uncrowded spots for snorkelling and swimming.

AIRLIE BEACH

Airlie Beach ❶ is the hub of the Whitsunday coast and your base for exploring the islands. It is a tourist town through and through, with accommodation options for all budgets (see page 105) and a vibrant dining scene. Numerous travel agencies, posing as information centres, will vie for your patronage with sailing, diving, cruising options and more.

You can stock up on camping provisions here and, to enjoy that last restaurant meal before going camping, head to **Deja Vu**, see ❶.

Shute Harbour

Shute Harbour ❷ is 10km (6 miles) east of Airlie Beach and is the home port for many of the vessels that service the resorts and islands. Whitsunday Island Camping Connections' 10-metre (30ft) barge, *Scamper*, designed to run up the beach to drop off campers and their gear, operates from here (book your passage: tel: 4946 6285; www.whitsunday camping.com.au; fares include drinking water and use of snorkelling gear; camping equipment available to hire). Book campsites and buy camping permits from Queensland Parks and Wildlife Service (tel: 131304; http://parks. nprsr.qld.gov.au).

The office is beside the water at the end of Shute Harbour Drive. Departure times from Shute Harbour are determined by tides, and usually there is one departure per day.

SOUTH MOLLE ISLAND

It takes just 15 minutes to transfer to the campsite at **Sandy Bay** ❸, on the southwestern corner of **South Molle**

The view from Hill Inlet

Island. Picnic tables and toilet facilities are available here. Be sure to keep your food well sealed, as native animals such as goannas, birds and possums are part of the experience, and they like to help themselves.

With 420ha (1,000 acres) of National Park, the island offers superb bushwalking. The walking tracks from Sandy Bay campsite to **Mount Jeffreys** and **Spion Kop** may be moderately challenging because of their length – the 11km (6.5-mile) return trip takes five hours – but you are rewarded with spectacular views. South Molle has a fascinating history of indigenous occupation, European settlement, grazing and tourism. The walk to Spion Kop passes a Ngaro quarry where the hillside is scattered with broken pieces of rock that were used to sharpen stone tools.

WHITSUNDAY ISLAND

The *Scamper* will return the next day (the time is dependent on tides) and take you on the 35-minute transfer to **Dugong Beach ❹**, your first camp on **Whitsunday Island**. From the beach, take the walking track to **Sawmill Beach** that leads on to **Whitsunday Peak**. This track may be one of the most challenging on the tour, reaching an elevation of 437m (1,400ft). It is a 5km (3-mile) return hike, and you should allow four hours total, to enjoy the views over the islands, turquoise waters and mainland. Steep, rocky hillsides support vine forest and open eucalypt forests, changing to grassland as you ascend. The unusual grass trees were once a source of food and tool material to the Ngaro, producing glue, fire sticks and spear handles, and yielding starch, nectar and grubs. If you are lucky you will spot white-bellied sea eagles and brahminy kites (red-backed sea eagles) soaring overhead. From May to September, watch for the blows and splashes of humpback whales that use these warm waters as a calving ground.

Whitehaven Beach

Be ready for your 45-minute *Scamper* transfer to **Whitehaven Beach ❺** on the opposite side of Whitsunday Island. Ask Whitsunday Island Camping Connections to drop off kayaks (charge) for you to explore the coastline further. Brilliant white silica sand stretching for over 7km (4 miles) greets you on impossibly perfect Whitehaven Beach. The beauty of camping overnight here is that you get to experience this paradise without the crowds. While the day-trippers are basking on the sand, take the opportunity to follow the **Solway Circuit**, a 40-minute return walk, or continue on the **Chance Bay** walk, which is 7km (4 miles) long (there and back) and takes around four hours. During this walk you will pass through beach scrub and grass-tree groves to cool cedar forests, and be rewarded with stunning views over Solway Passage to Haslewood Island and south to Hamilton and Pentecost islands.

Airlie Beach marina

Kayak to Tongue Bay

On the afternoon of the fourth day, take to the water in your kayak and listen for the exhalations of turtles (six of the world's seven marine species are found in the Whitsundays' waters) as you paddle 6km (4 miles) north to **Tongue Bay ❻**. Here you can tackle the **Tongue Point** walk, 3km (2 miles), which takes two hours return, to drink in breathtaking views of Whitehaven Beach from **Hill Inlet lookout**. As you paddle back to Whitehaven Beach camp, explore the rich mangrove forests that flourish along the shoreline.

Whitsunday resorts

Camping is not for everyone, and although just a handful of the 74 Whitsunday Islands are home to holiday resorts, these islands are the focus of most of the Whitsunday hype. Resorts range from the super-luxurious Hayman Island (www.hayman.com.au) to the more backpacker-friendly Barefoot Lodge Long Island (www.barefootlodge.com.au), and the South Molle Island Resort (koala adventures.com/south-molle-island). Somewhere between these extremes lie the intimate eco-based luxury of Paradise Bay (www.paradisebay.com.au) on Long Island, the family friendly resorts of Daydream Island (www.daydreamisland.com) and Lindeman Island (www.lindeman-island-whitsundays.com.au), and the large and popular Hamilton Island (www.hamiltonisland.com.au). Many of these resorts can be visited as a day guest from Airlie Beach or Shute Harbour, with connections operated by Cruise Whitsundays (www.cruisewhitsundays.com).and their more backpacker-orientated subsidiary Awesome Adventures OZ (www.awesomeoz.com).

RETURN TO AIRLIE BEACH

On the morning of the fifth day, catch the one-hour *Scamper* transfer back to Shute Harbour and then reward yourself with dinner at **Capers at the Beach** (see page 116) in Airlie Beach. Alternatively, the Whitsundays are a great place to learn to sail, charter or skipper your own boat (see page 23). Scuba-diving is very popular here too (see page 27), with pristine coral reefs teeming with marine life. Check out www.tourismwhitsundays. com.au for a taste of what else is on offer.

Food and Drink

❶ DEJA VU

Golden Orchid Drive, Airlie Beach; tel: 4948 4309; www.dejavurestaurant.com. au; Wed–Sat noon–2.30pm, 6–9pm, Sun from 12.30pm; $$$
This intimate poolside restaurant blends Indian, Mediterranean and Asian influences with fine Queensland produce. Whole Thai reef fish, signature goat curry and lamb rack with dolmades are just a small selection from the creative menu.

Cairns seafront

CAIRNS

Cairns is a tropical outpost blessed with myriad natural charms and with more than a hint of colonial character. Set off on this leisurely stroll to capture some of the South Pacific magic that is too easily missed by those who rush straight to the reef.

DISTANCE: 6.5km (4 miles), not including Red Arrow Circuit
TIME: A half-day
START: Marlin Marina
END: Botanic Gardens
POINTS TO NOTE: Cairns Airport has regular flights direct from most state capitals, and long-distance buses connect Cairns with Brisbane and all major stops in between. Queensland Rail (www.queenslandrailtravel.com. au) runs a service five times a week between Brisbane and Cairns.

Cairns preserves much of its early beginnings as a port for inland goldfields and a centre for sugar-cane production, with several examples of tropical colonial architecture. Other industries have succeeded here, but none more so than the Great Barrier Reef tourism that powers the town today. Cairns is at its busiest in the southern states' winter holidays, when Melbournians and Sydneysiders come flocking in their thousands to escape the chill.

When Captain James Cook sailed past in 1770, gingerly negotiating the same offshore coral reefs that now pull in thousands of his fellow curious countrymen (and women), the hills and coastal flats around present-day Cairns were the home to several tribes of the Djabugay language group, including the Yidinji people. Today, local indigenous culture is vibrant and celebrated throughout the region.

MARLIN MARINA

Start at **Marlin Marina ❶**, the berth for the massive wave-piercing catamarans that whisk people to the coral reefs every day. At the **Reef Fleet Terminal** the major cruise operators are represented, making this a good place to peruse what is on offer. Breakfast here at the **Al Porto Café Restaurant**, while watching the comings and goings of the waterfront, see ❶.

A boardwalk hugs the Trinity Inlet shoreline fronting the marina. The two major jetties that embrace the marina are open to all, though it is prohibited

The exterior of Cairns Regional Gallery

to enter the smaller jetties where private craft are moored. Take a look at what the fishermen are catching as you wander north along the boardwalk with the boats on your right. To the left, the upmarket Shangri-La Hotel occupies the upper floors of **The Pier** complex. An elevated veranda skirts the complex and is home to numerous restaurants and bars. Continue on to **Marina Point**, the

Cairns Swimming Lagoon   *In Cairns Regional Gallery*

location of the **Cairns Yacht Club** and the very popular **Salt House** (see page 118), a huge outdoor restaurant and bar, offering panoramas of the harbour, city and the blue-green hills of Yarrabah.

CAIRNS SWIMMING LAGOON

When you reach the Cairns Harbour wall, turn left and follow the sweeping path along the shore. At high tide, the water laps the narrow sandy beach and when it recedes, Cairns' famous mud-flats are exposed. The mud is a feeding platter for hundreds of water birds, some of which migrate from as far away as Siberia, and even the occasional crocodile (keep your eyes peeled).

Cairns is blessed with year-round warm temperatures, ranging from 25–33°C (77–91°F), but in summer, humidity often gets extremely high, and it can be huge relief to see the metal fish spraying water, which herald the **Cairns Swimming Lagoon ❷** (Thur–Tue 6am–10pm, Wed noon–10pm, free). Swimming in the stinger-free clear waters of this vast salt-water pool and lying around on the mani-cured lawns are virtually mandatory for all visitors, but you might also want to check out *The Herd*, a delightful granite sculpture at the tail end of the lagoon.

CULTURAL CAIRNS

Cross the **Esplanade** here and head along Shields Street to the **Cairns Regional Gallery ❸** (corner of Shields and Abbott streets; www.cairnsregional gallery.com.au; Mon–Fri 9am–5pm, Sat 10am–5pm, Sun 10am–2pm; charge). Exhibits include the gallery's collection of international and Australian artists – with a particular focus on indigenous artists and those from the tropical north – plus visiting exhibitions.

Walk westwards on Shields Street to the intersection with Lake Street where the **Cairns Museum ❹** (corner Shields and Lake streets; Mon–Sat 10am–4pm; charge) occupies the balconied former School of Arts building. At the time of writing the museum was closed for a major refurbishment, but check the web-site for updates if you're interested in exploring some engaging exhibits.

Make your way back along Shields Street and turn right on Abbott Street. On the left-hand side of the street you pass several heritage buildings con-verted to a variety of modern uses: the **Courthouse Hotel** was once the Cairns courthouse, but occupying its 1882 building, the **Cairns Post** still produces the local newspapers. Turn left at Spence Street to head back to the Esplanade, but not before grabbing a quality cup of something coffee-fla-voured at **Bang and Grind**, see ❷.

CAIRNS WILDLIFE DOME

On the right is the **Reef Casino**, the top floor of which houses the **Cairns Wild-life Dome ❺** (www.cairnsdome.com. au; daily 9am–8pm; charge). Star bill-

Monument to the 75th anniversary of the founding of the RAAF

ing here goes to Goliath, the 4-metre (13ft) estuarine crocodile, but there are also bird shows, koalas and more. Set aside about an hour to explore – more for feeding times – although remember your ticket is valid for five days so you can return any time.

Turn left at the Esplanade, where you will soon see the helpful **Cairns & Tropical North Visitor Information Centre** (51 The Esplanade; www.cairnsgreat barrierreef.org.au Mon–Fri 8.30am–6pm, Sat–Sun 10am–6pm).

NIGHT MARKETS

Cross over Shields Street, to the **Night Markets** (daily 5–11pm), a raggedy collection of food and merchandise stalls that swings into life at dusk. Cross the Esplanade, skirt the northwestern shore of the Lagoon and join the **Cairns Foreshore Promenade**.

CAIRNS FORESHORE PROMENADE

The promenade hugs the shoreline almost to the airport. During the day, shade is available, but scarce, so carry plenty of water. Information panels along the walk describe the history and ecology of the region. Two artillery pieces flank the **Cairns War Memorial Cenotaph ❻**, built to honour men from Cairns who died in World War I. The clock faces permanently show 4.28am, the time at which the ANZAC landing at Gallipoli began on 25 April 1915.

Continue along the promenade, through **Muddy's Playground**, a wet and wild playground for little kids with a café where you can grab a cool drink.

Nearby, atop a tall plinth, is a tiny commemorative model of a **Catalina flying boat ❼**, a one-time frequent visitor to Trinity Inlet during World War II. From their base at Cairns, these remarkable aircraft flew patrols of up to 24 hours in duration, locating and attacking ships of the Japanese fleet.

Pass behind the children's playground pirate ship as the path swings inland and continue north along the Esplanade as it sweeps around to the left and turns into Lily Street. Continue down Lily Street, cross busy Sheridan Street at the lights and turn right, walking one block down Sheridan. Turn left into Arthur Street (which becomes Greenslopes Street), and then go over the railway crossing and Lily Creek bridge.

On the next corner is **Cominos House ❽** (Mon–Fri 9am–5pm), a colonial-style home on stilts that was the residence of one of Cairns's earliest settler families until 1988. Relocated from its original Abbott Street site, it has been adapted into an environmental and arts centre.

BOTANIC GARDENS

Opposite and on your right is a path leading into the **Cairns Botanic Gardens ❾** (Mon–Fri 7.30am–5.30pm, Sat–Sun 8.30am–5.30pm; free). Enter the shady gardens and cross the nar-

Shopping at the night markets　　　　*Goliath the crocodile at the Cairns Wildlife Dome*

row footbridge over the mangrove-lined Saltwater Creek. Just after the crossing, take the right fork on the path and then the left fork a little further on. The dense bush on your left closely represents the rainforest before European settlement, with huge swamp paperbarks and other native trees (many of them labelled).

You'll soon emerge onto Collins Avenue opposite the **Tanks Art Centre** 🔟 (www.tanksartscentre.com; Mon–Fri 9am–4.30pm; free gallery entry), an extraordinary contemporary art and performance facility housed in three massive World War II oil-storage tanks. The tanks were completed for the Royal Australian Navy in 1944 and camouflaged here to store crude oil for the war effort. In the early 1990s, talk of removing the tanks caused a massive outcry, so it was decided to redevelop the site into this unique and heritage-listed arts space.

If you have the energy, continue up the hill past the tanks to the **Mount Whitfield Conservation Park** 🔟 and the **Red Arrow Circuit** (1.5km/1 mile). There are some steep sections to this track, but the rewards include walking through virgin rainforest and sweeping views over Cairns and Trinity Bay.

Walking west on Collins Avenue, you soon reach the original Botanic Gardens entrance and the information centre, toilets, orchid house and **Botanic Gardens Restaurant/Cafe**, which is the perfect place for lunch, see ❸. Afterwards you could walk it off on the **Rainforest Boardwalk**, starting opposite the main entrance, through lush tropical rainforest. From here, the best way to return is to catch a bus on Collins Avenue. There is a stop right outside the original entrance. Or wander back through the gardens and catch a bus from Sheridan Street. Otherwise, call a taxi (tel: 131008 for Black & White taxis).

Food and Drink

❶ AL PORTO CAFÉ RESTAURANT
1 Spence Street; tel: 4031 6222; www.al portocairns.com; daily 6.30am–3pm; $$
At the wharf end of the Reef Fleet Terminal, Al Porto serves breakfast until they close the doors. There are tropical-fruit salads, yoghurt and toasted muesli, and eggs several ways. Steak, pasta, seafood and wine are available for lunch.

❷ BANG AND GRIND
8/14 Spence St, tel 4051 7770; daily 6am-4pm $
One of Far North Queensland's craft coffee outlets that is delighting latte loving hipsters from further south (and anyone else who appreciates a good cup of caffeine).

❸ BOTANIC GARDENS RESTAURANT/ CAFE
Collins Avenue; tel: 4053 7087; www.cafe botanic.com.au; daily 7am–4.30pm; $
Enjoy a light salad, or maybe one of the sinfully sticky waffles, under a canopy of tropical rainforest trees.

Skyrail takes you over the rainforest

KURANDA CIRCUIT

Silently glide over a green sea of trees on the award-winning Skyrail Rainforest Cableway to pretty Kuranda, situated on the lush highlands above Cairns. Kuranda is encircled by rainforest and renowned for arts, crafts and its alternative lifestyle.

DISTANCE: 44.5km (27 miles) of which 3km (2 miles) is on foot
TIME: A full day
START: Caravonica Terminal
END: Freshwater Railway Station
POINTS TO NOTE: Book ahead through your accommodation or directly with Skyrail (www.skyrail.com.au) or Kuranda Scenic Railway (www.ksr.com.au). Both offer railway/cableway packages. You can also get bus transfers from your accommodation to either terminal and from one terminal to the other (handy if you self-drive). Book your departure time for 9am; the last train leaves Kuranda at 3.30pm. This tour can also be done by ascending on the railway and returning on the cableway, or just doing a round trip on either the cableway or railway. Check out available packages, which allow you to bundle your Skyrail booking with entry to some of Kuranda's attractions.

Your journey on the **Skyrail Rainforest Cableway** launches from **Caravonica Terminal ❶** in Smithfield (corner of Cairns Western Arterial Road and Captain Cook Highway), a 15-minute drive north of Cairns along the Captain Cook Highway. The 7.5km (4.5-mile) aerial journey takes approximately 1.5 hours, including two informative stops along the way where you can get out and explore the rainforest of **Barron Gorge National Park**.

SKYRAIL RAINFOREST RAILWAY

As you set off from Caravonica Terminal and skim above the **McAlister Range**, the dense canopy of World Heritage tropical rainforest – the most ancient 'old-growth' tropical rainforest on Earth and home to an amazing diversity of life – stretches out below. The rainforest actually extends over 500km (300 miles) along the north Queensland coastline. Look back for a spectacular view of Cairns out to the Coral Sea. At the first stop, at **Red Peak ❷**, you can join the complimentary ranger-guided walks along a short boardwalk surrounded by giant ferns, lush palms and towering trees. Together with interpretive signs,

Barron Gorge

the rangers will help you identify some of the rainforest's more interesting and unusual species. Re-board a gondola for the short journey to the second stop.

Barron Falls

At **Barron Falls** ❸ you disembark onto a boardwalk that leads to three lookouts providing breathtaking forest-framed views of the mighty gorge and falls. Especially impressive when the Barron is in full flood during the wet season (Dec–Mar), the flow drastically reduces for the rest of the year (so do not be put off if your visit coincides with some rain, as this is when the rainforest is at its very best, shrouded in mist and streaked with thundering waterfalls). Here you will find the **Rainforest Interpretation Centre**, with interactive displays, videos and information that will help unravel some of the mysteries of this fascinating ecosystem. Re-board a gondola for the final 10-minute journey over the rainforest and the impressive **Barron River** to Kuranda village.

KURANDA

Skyrail's Kuranda terminal is adjacent to the **Kuranda Railway Station**, from where it is just a short wander along Coondoo Street to heart of gorgeous **Kuranda village** ❹. It is exceedingly easy to lose several hours leisurely strolling among the shops, cafés and wildlife attractions. Discovered in the 1960s by hippies who wanted to live an alternative lifestyle in idyllic surroundings, the rainforest village continues to attract legions of talented artists and craftspeople today, hence the plethora of bustling markets.

There are plenty of places for a break, such as the **Windmill Café**,

The Kuranda Scenic Railway

see ❶, on Coondoo Street, which is good for a coffee and a bagel. Where Coondoo intersects with Therwine Street you will see **Centenary Park**, home to the very helpful **Kuranda Visitor Information Centre** (www.kuranda.org). From here you can start on an easy 3km (2-mile) circuit walk that combines the Jumrum Creek, Jungle Walk and River Walk trails.

Markets

Turn right turn from Coondoo Street and head along Therwine Street. On the right are the **Original Kuranda Rainforest Markets** ❹ (corner Therwine and Thooree streets; daily 9am–3pm), a village within a village, with exclusive, locally made fashions, crafts and foods. Diagonally across the road are the **Heritage Markets** (Rob Veivers Drive; www.kurandamarkets.com; daily 9.30am–3.30pm), with yet more souvenirs and fashions, but also featuring a couple of wildlife attractions. You can enjoy lunch at one of Kuranda's oldest establishments, **Frogs Restaurant**, see ❷. The market areas overflow with crafts and produce; kangaroo, toad and crocodile products swamp the sidewalks. The rainforest surrounding Kuranda has been home to the Djabugay people for over 10,000 years, making it also a popular spot to pick up a souvenir didgeridoo.

Kuranda attractions

At the rear of the Heritage Markets is **BirdWorld Kuranda** ❸ (www.birdworld-kuranda.com; daily 9am–4pm; charge), home to the largest single collection of free-flying birds in Australia. Over 75 species of the most spectacular birds from all corners of the planet are on display here, including Australia's endangered, flightless giant – the cassowary.

A walkway links BirdWorld to two more wildlife attractions. The **Australian Butterfly Sanctuary** ❻ (8 Rob Veivers Drive; www.australianbutterflies.com; daily 9.45am–4pm; charge) is the largest butterfly enclosure in Australia. The flight aviary is home to some 2,000 tropical butterflies, including the spectacular Cairns birdwing. On the other side of BirdWorld is **Kuranda Koala Gardens** ❼ (www.koalagardens.com; daily 9am–4pm; charge), where you can get your photo taken cuddling a koala, watch wombats and kangaroos, spot a

Around the Scenic Railway · *In the rainforest village of Kuranda*

freshwater crocodile and brave the walk-through snake house.

Can't get enough of critters? Check out the **Australian Venom Zoo** (8 Coondoo Street; www.tarantulas.com.au; daily 10am–4pm; charge), which breeds and displays venomous spiders, snakes and insects. Just down the road, **BatReach** (Jungle Walk, Coondoo Street; Tue–Fri and Sun 10.30am–2.30pm; admission by donation) is a volunteer-operated rescue and rehabilitation centre for injured and orphaned flying foxes and micro bats.

While you're back on Coondoo Street you can sample a delicious range of homemade cakes and pastries at **The Coffee Kitchen**, see ❸.

KURANDA SCENIC RAILWAY

Make your way back to Kuranda Railway Station for the 3.30pm departure of the **Kuranda Scenic Railway** ❺, a 90-minute journey through deep ravines and lush rainforest and past spectacular waterfalls. Constructed between 1882 and 1891, the railway is a tremendous feat of engineering. Hundreds of men were employed to build the 15 hand-dug tunnels and 37 bridges, and at least 23 workers died before the railway opened up the rich Atherton Tablelands to agriculture and later to tourism.

There is a brief photo stop at the station overlooking **Barron Falls** to see the river plunge (or trickle, depending on the time of year) from its placid Kuranda reaches into the gorge. The train also slows over a picturesque steep gully as it crosses **Stoney Creek Bridge**, with a backdrop of one of the region's most spectacular waterfalls. Eventually you will arrive at **Freshwater Railway Station** to catch your transfer bus back to Cairns or the Skyrail terminal.

Food and Drink

❶ WINDMILL CAFÉ

25 Coondoo Street; tel: 4093 9466; daily 9am–4pm; $

Conveniently located on the corner as you walk up the hill from Skyrail, this café serves bagels and sandwiches, luscious cakes, coffee and freshly squeezed juices.

❷ FROGS RESTAURANT

2/4 Rob Veivers Drive; tel: 4093 8952; www.frogsrestaurant.com.au; daily 9.30am–4pm; $$

Built in 1923, and one of Kuranda's first cafés, this licensed restaurant has recently relocated to the Heritage Markets, where you can sit on the verandah with superb rainforest views and enjoy an extensive menu ranging from gourmet pizzas to fresh local barramundi.

❸ THE COFFEE KITCHEN

20 Coondoo Street; tel: 4093 9169; daily 7.30am–3pm; $

Grab a table inside or out under a tree and choose from an assortment of freshly baked, handmade baguettes, pastries and cakes.

PORT DOUGLAS AND MOSSMAN GORGE

Travel north from Cairns along one of Australia's most spectacular coastal roads with dramatic views of the Coral Sea. Discover the seaside towns of Port Douglas and Palm Cove, and float in the crystal-clear waters of Mossman Gorge.

DISTANCE: 182km (110 miles)
TIME: A full day
START/END: Cairns
POINTS TO NOTE: You will need a car for this trip, and don't forget your swimming gear. This tour can be combined with Route 13; Daintree village is a 35km (21-mile) drive north of Mossman.

This journey past Cairns's northern beaches unveils golden swathes of palm-fringed sand along 26km (16 miles of unspoilt shoreline, fronted by the Coral Sea and backed by mountains. Small, laid-back villages rest lazily beside the sea. Further on, the larger, glitzier towns of Palm Cove and Port Douglas lure an eclectic crowd of backpackers, botoxed retirees and a few well-heeled international visitors.

TO PORT DOUGLAS

Make an early start from Cairns and head north on the Captain Cook High-way for 67km (40 miles) to Port Douglas. As you leave Cairns you will pass the **Skyrail Rainforest Cableway** (see page 76) to Kuranda and **Tjapukai Cultural Park** (www.tjapukai.com. au; daily 9am–5pm, evening show 7–10pm; charge) a place that's ensuring a 40,000-year-old culture remains alive and which leads visitors through a Dreamtime journey of creation with traditional dance, music and legends. Branching off the highway to the east are roads leading to serene beachside villages such as **Yorkeys Knob, Trinity Beach, Palm Cove** and **Ellis Beach**. At **Palm Cove** (see page 83), look out for **Cairns Tropical Zoo** (www.cairns tropicalzoo.com.au; daily 8.30am–4pm; charge), which offers myriad animal-related activities and encounters. After Wangetti Beach, pause at **Rex Lookout** to take in the panoramic views.

Wildlife Habitat

Just before the entrance to Port Douglas is the **Wildlife Habitat** ❶ (Corner Captain Cook Highway and Port Douglas Road; www.wildlifehabitat.com.au; daily

Looking over Port Douglas

8am–5pm; charge), where you can experience **Breakfast with the Birds**, see , and then enjoy presentations on the local ecology of wetlands, rainforest and grasslands.

PORT DOUGLAS

From here it is only 6km (3.5 miles) to the heart of **Port Douglas** ❷ (or Port, as it's known to the locals). Not very long ago, Port Douglas was a sleepy seaside settlement. Today, it has been transformed into a fashionable tropical holiday resort, with the whole spectrum of tourist accommodation, award-winning restaurants, beautiful galleries and upmarket shopping. Fortunately, the transition has not entirely robbed Port Douglas of its natural charm.

The approach from the main road is lined by an avenue of about 450 huge African oil palms; as many again are planted around the **Sheraton Mirage Resort** and the **Marina Mirage**. They form part of the extravagant vision of former multi-millionaire Christopher Skase, who transplanted the trees here at a cost of about A$1,500 each. Skase went spectacularly bust in a series of media and leisure ventures in the late 1980s; happily, Port Douglas fared better and has continued to prosper.

Macrossan Street
The main drag, **Macrossan Street**, is lined with a colourful array of shops, eateries and restaurants, and is well worth a wander. The sidewalks are thronged with casual pedestrians, who seem to have all the time (and money) in the world. With a core population of approximately 4,000 people, the town also sports a world-class marina and international-standard golf courses.

At the western end of Macrossan Street (on the corner with Wharf Street),

A furry face at Cairns Tropical Zoo

the Court House Hotel is the oldest pub in town (in operation since 1878), now home to **The Wharf Street Bistro**, (see page 119). Across the road is **Anzac Park**, which overflows with market stalls on Sunday mornings (8am–midday), selling arts and crafts as well as fresh food.

Four Mile Beach

Running along the southeastern side of the peninsula, **Four Mile Beach ❸** is the town's prime asset: a long, lonely stretch of sand, backed by palm trees, with no signs of development (houses are neatly hidden behind the palms). Swimming is reasonably safe (ask the life guards for guidance), but stay inside the stinger nets in stinger season (Oct–May, see page 26).

TO MOSSMAN GORGE

Take the main road out of Port Douglas back to the Captain Cook Highway. Turn right for the 26km (16-mile) drive north to Mossman. As you climb up towards the misty mountains, shrouded in greenery, the air becomes cooler and filled with the refreshing scent of the rainforest. Turn left at Mossman and follow the signs for 5km (3 miles) to Mossman Gorge.

On the way to the gorge is the **Kuku Yalanji Dreamtime Centre ❹** (www.yalanji.com.au; Mon–Fri 8.30am–5pm, Sat 8.30am–1pm). The Kuku Yalanji are the indigenous inhabitants of this land, which stretches from around Cooktown in the north to near Chilla-

goe in the west and Port Douglas in the south. The centre's free Aboriginal Art Gallery is well worth a browse. They also offer 90-minute guided walks (charge) around Mossman Gorge.

MOSSMAN GORGE

Make your way to the car park for spectacular **Mossman Gorge ❺**. Remember to pack your swimming gear if you want to experience the crystal waters of the Mossman River; swimming here is safe and crocodile-free as long as you exercise caution. The short **River Circuit track**

In Mossman Gorge   *Lounging on Palm Cove's beach*

(10 minutes) takes you to a viewing plat-form over the river, but if you would like to escape the crowds, take the 3km (2-mile) **Rainforest Circuit track** (approximately one hour return). For a really different experience, check out the River Snorkel-ling tours offered by Back Country Bliss (www.backcountrybliss.com.au). These tours involve a three-hour swim along the Mossman River, through the Daintree Rainforest, as your guide explains the symbiotic relationship between the rain-forest and the reef. Be warned – most other rivers around here are not croc free, so don't try and do this on your own.

PALM COVE

Head back along the Captain Cook High-way towards Cairns. After about 50km (30 miles) turn left for **Palm Cove ❻**, a beachside development where the cob-bled streets and 500-year-old melaleuca trees bestow a tranquil mood. This spot is about sheer relaxation, pampering and fine-dining. For afternoon tea overlooking the sea, try **Ando's Bar & Grill**, see ❷. From here it is a 30-minute drive back to Cairns on the Captain Cook Highway.

Food and Drink

❶ BREAKFAST WITH THE BIRDS

Wildlife Habitat, corner Captain Cook Highway and Port Douglas Road; tel: 4099 3235; www.wildlifehabitat.com.au; daily 8–10.30am; $$$

Enjoy a full buffet breakfast with fruits, pastries, cereals and hot food from the BBQ while immersing yourself in the wetlands environment and being joined by a throng of birds that wander freely amid the tables.

❷ ANDO'S BAR & GRILL

6/139 Williams Esplanade, Palm Cove; tel: 4059 2234; daily 7am–10pm; $$

In a divine setting with a great outlook over the Coral Sea, Ando's is all about relaxed dining. Just enjoy a coffee or cool drink in the sea breeze, savour one of their delicious pizzas or tackle the popular Reef and Beef classic meal.

Daintree River from above

DAINTREE AND CAPE TRIBULATION

Take a full day to drive through the spectacular Wet Tropics and Daintree World Heritage area. Spot crocs on the river, wander boardwalks through mangroves, take a dip at Mason's swimming hole and enjoy sprawling, deserted beaches.

DISTANCE: 44km (26 miles)
TIME: A full day
START: Daintree
END: Cape Tribulation
POINTS TO NOTE: Daintree is 110km (66 miles) north of Cairns via Mossman; alternatively, this route could easily be linked with Route 12. A car is needed for this route and you will need to bring cash to pay for the ferry across the river. Consider overnighting in the rainforest to maximise your wilderness experience with adventures such as nocturnal wildlife walks and jungle surfing through the canopy. Book your morning Daintree River cruise in advance.

The Daintree River, one of the longest rivers on Australia's East Coast, was named by George Elphinstone Dalrymple after his friend Richard Daintree, an English geologist. Dalrymple wrote 'No river in North Australia possesses surroundings combining so much of distant mountain grandeur with local beauty and wealth of vegetation.'

DAINTREE

Daintree ❶ is a tiny, historic village on the southern bank of the scenic Daintree River overlooked by Queensland's third-highest mountain, **Thornton Peak** (1,374m/4,507ft). It's a picturesque setting, originally the base for cedar-getters who came to log prized red cedar, which once flourished in the area. There's not much more here to detain you other than the **Daintree Village General Store**, see ❶, which can supply you with information on the area and sell tickets for a Daintree River Cruise if you have not already booked.

River cruises

Daintree River cruises take place on several different sections of the river. The tours take you up or downstream, through narrow reaches lined with mangroves and rainforests that are rich in wildlife. It is unusual not to spot a crocodile from a safe distance, especially in the cooler months when the huge reptiles leave the water to sun themselves on the riverbank. The depar-

Board the Daintree Ferry

ture jetty for many of the river cruises is a short downhill stroll from the Daintree Village General Store. Operators include Crocodile Express (www.daintreeconnection.com.au; daily one-hour cruises 8.30am–5pm), Bruce Belcher's Daintree River Cruises (www.daintreerivercruises.com.au; daily one-hour cruises; www.daintreerivertours.com.au; daily dawn and evening cruises, plus full- and half-day trips).

Daintree Ferry

Drive east along Daintree Road for 10km (6 miles) to the turnoff to the **Daintree Ferry ❷** (6am–midnight; charge). On the other side of the two-minute crossing, a good sealed road tunnels through overhanging trees all the way to Cape Tribulation. Take care on the narrow, winding stretches that hug the cliff edges. Speed humps are placed along the road to slow traffic in areas where southern cassowaries – large, flightless birds that can be very aggressive towards humans – may be encountered. Cassowaries undertake a key role in the rainforest, spreading tree seeds after they have digested the fruit. Sadly it is quite rare to observe these extraordinary animals in the wild, but if you do see one, it is best to keep your distance, particularly if they are in a family group with young (and definitely don't get in between the adults and the chicks, as they are aggressively protective parents).

After 8km (5 miles) you reach the **Alexandra Range Lookout**, with sweeping views back to the south, across the wide mouth of the Daintree River, to Snapper Island and the sugar-cane fields and ranges beyond.

Daintree Discovery Centre

A little further north, pull over at the **Daintree Discovery Centre** ❸ (www. daintree-rec.com.au; daily 8.30am–5pm; charge). This award-wining interpretive centre provides a rainforest booklet and comprehensive audio guides that together give you an excellent insight into what you see as you self-guide along the low-impact boardwalk and ascend the breathtaking heights of the Canopy Tower. Standing 23m (76ft) tall, and featuring five viewing platforms, the tower provides a fantastic experience for photographers, botany enthusiasts and bird-watchers alike.

TO CAPE TRIBULATION

Drive further north, passing the **Cow Bay Hotel Motel** and then **Thornton Beach**, where you can stop for a stroll along this peaceful stretch of sand backed by dense rainforest. You can walk to the mouth of **Cooper Creek**, one of Australia's richest mangrove ecosystems (but watch out for crocodiles).

Continue north to reach the **Marrdja Boardwalk** ❹, a short (30-minute) loop walk beside a running rocky stream, through lush rainforest and mangroves. A little further north again is **Mason's Café, Store and Tours** (Cape Tribulation Road; www.masonstours. com.au), which offers guided day and night walks, 4WD tours and croc-spotting (as well as great milkshakes and food). If you want to cool down, a little path behind the store leads to **Mason's swimming hole**, a lovely spot where you can rope-swing into the cool water of Myall Creek.

CAPE TRIBULATION

It is just a short drive from Mason's Café to **Cape Tribulation** ❺. The cape was so named by Captain Cook in 1770,

---

Old-growth rainforest

The tropical rainforest stretching from just north of Cairns through Cape Tribulation and on to Cooktown is around 110 million years old, and a remnant of the extensive forest that used to cover most of Australia and, before that, Gondwanaland. With this extraordinary ancestry, the north Queensland rainforest boasts the highest number of endemic species in the world, and is rightfully recognised and protected within the Wet Tropics World Heritage Area. Some of the most accessible rainforest is in the Daintree National Park, showcased by the Daintree Discovery Centre.

Experiencing the rainforest from a zipline

'because here began all our troubles'. Just after the 'Welcome to Cape Tribulation' sign, turn right into the **Dubuji Visitor Area** and walk the easy 1km (0.65-mile) boardwalk loop around freshwater swamps and mangroves, which also has access to the expansive **Myall Beach**.

Cape Tribulation consists only of a small cluster of shops, including a pharmacy, small supermarket and PK's Jungle Village, a backpackers' resort with a rowdy bar. Continue 1km (0.65 mile) north to **Kulki–Cape Tribulation Beach**, where there is an easy pathway to an elevated lookout over Cape Tribulation Beach and a rough track over the headland to Myall Beach. These two magnificent, picture-postcard beaches, where golden sands and azure waters rim the deep-green rainforest, are the main drawcard and the climax of the drive. Do not be alarmed by the harmless goannas (large monitor lizards) which hang out here scavenging from picnickers.

For the adventurous, **Jungle Surfing Canopy Tours** (Cape Tribulation; www.junglesurfing.com.au; daily 7.45am–3.30pm; charge) offer an exhilarating way to experience the rainforest from above, on flying-fox ziplines, stopping at five tree platforms to take in the bird's-eye views.

If you want to escape the cape and hit the coral, from the Daintree/Cape Tribulation area it is only 30–40 minutes by boat to the Great Barrier Reef. Snorkelling and diving trips are run by Ocean Safari (www.oceansafari.com.au).

From here, the road north is unsealed and only accessible by 4WD. It is approximately 2.5 hours' drive south from Cape Tribulation to Cairns – if you're looking to grab a bite to eat before heading back, check out **Whet Café and Bar**, see ❷, in Cape Tribulation, a real culinary surprise in the midst of the jungle.

Food and Drink

❶ DAINTREE VILLAGE GENERAL STORE AND RESTAURANT
Daintree; tel: 4098 6146; daily 8am–7.30pm; $$
Lunch and dinner options featuring local fauna include crocodile burgers and pan-fried locally caught barramundi. Also on offer is a selection of freshly baked cakes and scones. BYO beer and wine can be bought at the general store.

❷ WHET CAFÉ AND BAR
Cape Tribulation Road, Cape Tribulation; tel: 4098 0007; www.whet.net.au; daily 11am–4pm, 6pm–8.30pm; $$
It's not easy finding fine dining this far north, but bucking this trend with sublime style are the crew behind Whet, who serve fabulous food and ensure it's accompanied with a fantastic atmosphere. Try the scallops and the barramundi.

The granite gorge in Davies Creek National Park

ATHERTON TABLELANDS

Discover the charm of the Atherton Tablelands, also known as the Cairns Highlands, on this two-day drive visiting a plateau of patchwork farms, volcanic lakes and tumbling waterfalls. On the way, sample some of the world's best coffee in Mareeba and overnight in historic Yungaburra.

DISTANCE: Day one to Yungaburra: 120km (72 miles); day two: 70km (42 miles)
TIME: Two days
START: Cairns
END: Crawford's Lookout
POINTS TO NOTE: You will need a car, and to stay overnight in Yungaburra (see page 109). For Kuranda see route 11. Instead of returning straight to Cairns at the end of the trip, you could carry on to Mission Beach, or visit some of the sights on the way to Cairns on that route (see page 94).

The Tablelands have long been known as the food bowl of the Tropics. Incorporating the townships of Mareeba, Atherton, Herberton, Ravenshoe, Millaa Millaa and Malanda, the region is renowned for its dairy products and for growing tea, coffee and sugar. Combine this bountiful larder with the invigorating natural beauty of fast-flowing waterfalls, pristine lakes and crystal streams, and you have a destination that revitalises the five senses. More

recently, the region has also become known for the quality of its mountain biking, with an extensive trail network being put into the forests around several of the Tableland towns, including a particularly good one near Davies Creek (see below) near Mareeba.

TO MAREEBA

Leave Cairns early and head northwest for 13km (8 miles) on the Captain Cook Highway to the Smithfield roundabout. Take the road to Kuranda (see page 77), a 30-minute winding drive through dense rainforest, and then follow the signs along the Kennedy Highway to Mareeba where the vegetation suddenly changes from rainforest to dry bush. The change is brought about by two factors: less rainfall and different soil. This heralds the beginning of the Atherton Tablelands: rich, rolling country, much of which is cultivated for agriculture.

Davies Creek National Park
After crossing Davies Creek, take the road on the left that leads to the **Davies**

Mareeba's landscape

Creek National Park **1**. This road is unsealed for 7km (4 miles) but is driveable in a conventional vehicle. The creek winds and falls through a granite gorge, providing the opportunity for a quick dip in dozens of rocky plunge pools. Beyond the campground there is a 2km (1-mile) walk to lookouts above **Davies Creek Falls**, and a short circuit track leads to a sandy picnic area where platypus may be spotted in the adjacent creek. Visitors with their own tents will find a great overnight spot at Lower Davies Creek camping area, which is accessible in a normal car for most of the year.

Head back out onto the Kennedy Highway, where the bush soon gives way to open farmland with mango, citrus and avocado orchards.

MAREEBA

Mareeba is the centre of the country's coffee-growing region, with over 75 percent of Australia's crop grown in the

Sampling the local coffee

district's fertile soils. Before you enter the town, about 5km (3 miles) from the Davies Creek turnoff, billboards direct you to **Jaques Coffee Plantation** ❷ (www.jaquescoffee.com). It is a 4km (2.5-mile) detour along Gilmore Road and well worth the effort for an insight into the coffee industry. Take a 20-minute tour (charge), followed by coffee- or liqueur-tasting, or just sample the produce at **Jaques Coffee Plantation Café**, see ❶.

Back on the highway, proceed into the town of **Mareeba**, where the **Coffee Works Experience** (136 Mason Street; www.coffeeworks.com.au) offers a coffee gift shop, coffee-tasting and a café. Tea-drinkers are also catered for!

TO ATHERTON

During World War II, the Atherton Tablelands area became a large military base, supporting between 100,000 and 300,000 troops from 140 different units, and Mareeba played a major role in the Battle of the Coral Sea. As you head south out of town on the Kennedy Highway there are a couple of historic collections. The first, after 5km (3 miles), is **Beck's Museum** ❸ (daily 10am–4pm; charge), the largest privately owned collection of war machines, planes and equipment in Queensland. Almost opposite is **Warbird Adventures** (Mareeba Airport; www.warbirdadventures.com.au; Wed–Sun 10am–4pm) where, for a price, you

can take to the skies in one of several ex-military aircraft. Helicopter flights are also available.

Continue your journey southwards towards **Walkamin**. Just before the town, the **Mount Uncle Distillery** (1819 Chewko Road; www.mtuncle.com; daily 10am–4.30pm) bottles and sells premium liqueurs and spirits distilled from tropical products such as coffee, limes and macadamia nuts. In the tiny township of Tolga, the **Tolga Woodworks Gallery and Café**, see ❷, has quite a reputation for home-style cooking and great coffee, as well as its crafts and furniture carved from rare and beautiful local timbers.

ATHERTON

Just five minutes down the road from Tolga is the town of **Atherton** ❹. The **Atherton Information Centre** (corner Main Street and Silo Road; www.athertoninformationcentre.com.au; daily 9am–5pm) provides maps and brochures and makes accommodation bookings. One of the town's attractions is the **Crystal Caves** (69 Main Street; www.crystalcaves.com.au; daily Mon–Fri 8.30am–5pm, Sat 8.30am–4pm, Sun 10am–4pm; charge), where a simulated cave houses a fine collection of crystals and fossils.

Curtain Fig Tree

From Atherton, follow the signs for Malanda, then take a left turn where the signpost indicates that it's 12km (7

Yungaburra's church   *On the shores of Lake Barrine*

miles) to Yungaburra. As you approach town, detour right to the **Curtain Fig Tree ❺**. Walk along the boardwalk that surrounds the tree and an interpretive display explains how this amazing natural sculpture was formed; a draped curtain of aerial roots first grew from the parasitic strangler fig, smothering the host tree, and the whole thing then fell sideways and the fig lowered its roots to the ground.

YUNGABURRA

Yungaburra ❻ is a historic village that has changed little since 1910 and boasts no fewer than 18 heritage-listed buildings. It makes a good restful overnight base, and the **Yungaburra Visitor Centre** (Cedar Street; www.yungaburra. com; daily Mon–Sat 9am–5pm, Sun 10am–4pm) can help with booking accommodation and dining options such as atmospheric **Nick's Swiss-Italian Restaurant and Yodeller's Bar**, see ❸. Also worth a look is the little hidden gem, the **Whistle Stop Café** (34 Cedar Street; tel: 4095 3913; daily 8.30am–3pm; $).

Crater Lakes National Park
Just to the east of town is **Lake Eacham**, a sparkling blue lake in a drowned volcanic crater fringed by lawn and surrounded by rainforest. Along with Lake Barrine, it is the main feature of **Crater Lakes National Park ❼**, and the perfect spot for an afternoon swim and

sunbathe. If you would like to stretch your legs, there is an easy 3km (2-mile) circuit around the lake. This is also a birdwatcher's paradise, with over 180 recorded species.

About 5km (3 miles) further northeast along the Gillies Highway is Lake Eacham's twin, **Lake Barrine**. The **Lake Edge Teahouse Restaurant**, see ❹ is an ideal breakfast spot for the second day of this route. After breakfast consider joining the **Lake Barrine Rainforest Cruise** (www.lakebarrine. com.au; charge). You will be able to spend 45 minutes cruising around the volcanic crater, listening to an informative wildlife commentary and sighting pelicans and other water birds, tortoises, fish and maybe – in the cooler months – amethystine pythons, the world's third-largest snake (growing up to 8.5 metres/28ft long) sunning themselves on branches. For good birdwatching and walking, there is a 5km (3-mile) track around the lake. A short stroll away from the restaurant are the giant twin kauri pines, estimated to be 1,000 years old.

MALANDA

From Lake Eacham, take the road south to **Malanda**, amid lush green pastures over red volcanic soil. The black-and-white Friesian cows grazing in these pastures each produce up to 30 litres (6.5 gallons) of milk a day. The **Malanda Dairy Centre** (8 James Street; www.

malandadairycentre.com; Mon–Fri 9.30am–3pm, Sat–Sun 9am–3pm; charge) runs factory tours (Mon–Fri before noon) and serves up a seriously good milkshake. If, after yesterday's focus on coffee, you are interested in finding out how tea is grown and processed, call into the **Nerada Tea Visitor Centre** (www.neradatea.com.au; daily 9am–4pm), just 10km (6 miles) outside of Malanda on the Glen Allyn Road. Back on the Malanda–Millaa Millaa Road, consider stopping at **Tarzali Lakes Aquaculture Centre for the Smokehouse Café**, see ⑤.

MILLAA MILLAA AND THE WATERFALL CIRCUIT

Continue along the highway for about 15km (9 miles) through farmland and rainforest to **Millaa Millaa** ❽, another dairy town, ringed by some of the Tablelands' most spectacular waterfalls. Enter the **Waterfall Circuit** by taking the Theresa Creek Road, 1km (0.65 mile) east of Millaa Millaa on the Palmerston Highway. The first stop is **Millaa Millaa Falls**, considered to be the perfect 'drop' of water and used in many shampoo commercials. Drive on to **Zillie Falls** (viewed from above) and **Ellinjaa Falls**.

Detour to Ravenshoe
From Millaa Millaa you could detour southwest 25km (15 miles) on the Old Palmerston Highway to **Ravenshoe** ❾,

Queensland's highest town at 920m (3,000ft). The **Ravenshoe Visitor Centre** (24 Moore Street; www.ravenshoe visitor centre.com.au; daily 9am–4pm, until 5pm May–Oct) can help with accommodation bookings and information on regional waterfalls and bushwalks. Within the visitor centre is also the **Nganyai Interpretive Centre**, showcasing the culture of the local Jirrbal people, whose language is one of the oldest spoken in the world.

RETURN TO CAIRNS

Homeward bound, take the Palmerston Highway east towards Innisfail. After 5km (3 miles) turn left on Brooks Road to **Mungalli Falls**. At the **Mungalli Creek Dairy** (251 Brooks Road, Millaa Millaa; www.mungallicreekdairy.com.au; daily 10am–4pm, closed 1 Feb–14 Mar) you can sample organic milk and cheese, and snack at the café. Brooks Road loops back to the Palmerston Highway, which descends through 14km (8 miles) of lush rainforest. At **Crawford's Lookout** ❿ there are views through a clearing down to the North Johnstone River, where you may spot white-water rafters. Here too is **Mamu Rainforest Canopy Walkway** (Wooroonooran National Park; http://nprsr.qld.gov.au/parks/mamu/; daily 9.30am–5.30pm; charge), where you can perch high amongst the rainforest canopy, looking down at the mighty North Johnstone River. These rainforest-clad mountains have cultural

Mungalli Falls

significance to the Mamu people, and informative signs explain the cultural history of the area. The return walk is 2.5km (1.5 miles), but count on at least an hour to enjoy the scenery properly along the 350m (1,150ft) of elevated walkway and from the 37m (120ft) observation tower with two viewing decks.

From here head 25km (16 miles) east to the Bruce Highway, where it's a straightforward run north for 87km (54 miles) back to Cairns. Alternatively, drive south for Mission Beach (see page 94).

Food and Drink

① JAQUES COFFEE PLANTATION CAFÉ & COFFEE SHOP
137 Leotta Road, Mareeba; tel: 4093 3284; www.jaquescoffee.com; daily 9am 5pm; $
Accompany the local brew with a selection of cookies, scones and cake, including tropical fruit cheesecakes.

② TOLGA WOODWORKS GALLERY AND CAFÉ
Kennedy Highway, Tolga; tel: 4095 4488; www.tolgawoodworks.com.au; daily 9am–5pm; $$
They make the most of locally grown produce, so try the Greek, Thai or Tuscan summer salads, along with breads and cakes and baked in a wood-fired oven and finish off with local coffee or leaf tea.

③ NICK'S SWISS-ITALIAN RESTAURANT AND YODELLER'S BAR
33 Gillies Highway, Yungaburra; tel: 4095 3330; www.nicksrestaurant.com.au; Tue–Sun 11.30am–3pm and 5.30–11pm; $$$

Choose from Nick's extensive Swiss-Italian menu, including pasta, rosti and Swiss bratwurst. Or if you prefer modern Australian, go with crumbed crocodile fillets or a jackaroo sirloin steak.

④ THE LAKE EDGE TEAHOUSE RESTAURANT
Lake Barrine, Gillies Highway, Yungaburra; tel: 4095 3847; www.lakebarrine.com.au; daily 9am–5pm; $$
Overlooking the lake, this place serves hearty breakfasts, light lunches, such as soups, salads and sandwiches, and all-day Devonshire teas.

⑤ SMOKEHOUSE CAFÉ
Tarzali Lakes Aquaculture Centre, Malanda–Millaa Millaa Road, Malanda; tel: 4097 2713; www.tarzalilakes.com; daily 10am–5pm; $$
Nestled on the shores of a lake stocked with barramundi, golden perch, jade perch and red claw (a delicious crustacean), it comes as no surprise that this café specialises in freshly prepared fish and, of course, a wide range of smoked treats; more surprising, however, is the extensive Thai menu.

Palm trees fringe Mission Beach

MISSION BEACH AND DUNK ISLAND

The first day of this driving route south of Cairns takes you to picturesque waterfalls on the way to the seaside village of Mission Beach. Day two is spent exploring Dunk Island, a tropical paradise for intrepid travellers.

DISTANCE: 157km (94 miles) from Cairns to Mission Beach
TIME: Two days
START: Cairns
END: Dunk Island
POINTS TO NOTE: On 3 February 2011, Tropical Cyclone Yasi ripped through parts of northern Queensland, leaving a trail of utter devastation in its wake. The eye of the storm passed directly over Mission Beach and Dunk Island. While Mission Beach has largely recovered, and has plenty of accommodation for all budgets, Dunk Island Resort is still closed (in ruins). You can, however, still visit the island as a day-tripper, or stay overnight in a tent – which will appeal to the adventurous, as will the fact that the beautiful island is almost devoid of tourists. You need a car for this route. Pack water and snacks.

As you travel south from Cairns, the route passes through spectacular mountain scenery and fertile fields of bananas and sugarcane to reach Australia's wettest towns. This is part of the 'Great Green Way', and here you will observe ever-increasing tropical greenery and experience the relaxed north Queensland lifestyle, where farming and fishing are dominant ways of life and where a cultural encounter involves having a yarn with locals in an old Queensland pub.

TO MISSION BEACH

Set out early from Cairns, travelling south on the Bruce Highway through Edmonton and Gordonvale. **Babinda**, about 60km (36 miles) south of Cairns, competes annually with Tully and Innisfail for the 'Golden Gumboot Award', which goes to the town recording the highest annual average rainfall, usually around 5m (over 15ft). The locals will tell you it rains for 11 months, and drips off the trees for the rest of the year. In fact, large amounts of rain tend to fall in a very short time, and there is plenty of tropical sunshine to power the unusually lush and diverse vegetation.

Falls in Paronella Park

Babinda Boulders

At Babinda, turn right and follow signs west for 8km (5 miles) to **Babinda Boulders ❶**, a Wet Tropics World Heritage Reserve with visitor facilities, located in the foothills of **Mt Bartle Frere**, Queensland's highest mountain at 1,622m (5,300ft). Take your swimming costume to the Boulders and walk the 850m/yd **Wonga Track Rainforest Circuit** to clear pools amidst giant tree ferns, moss-covered boulders and towering trees. The short **Devils Pool Walk** is another lovely stroll through the rainforest to viewing platforms and cascading pools. This entire area is a popular swimming spot for locals and tourists, but stick to the marked swimming areas and exercise care, as people have drowned at Devils Pool.

Josephine Falls

Continue south on the Bruce Highway, and after 9km (5.5 miles) take a right turn to **Josephine Falls ❷**. This is an 8km (5-mile) detour from the highway, and 10 minutes' walk through the rainforest will reward you with some of the most beautiful waterfalls in Queensland. The tumbling icy waters have been used in many television commercials, and you can swim here.

Innisfail and Paronella Park

The sugar town of **Innisfail** is another 13km (8 miles) further south. Sitting at the junction of the North Johnstone and South Johnstone rivers, Innisfail is

On Dunk Island's jetty

the no-fuss service hub for the region. From Innisfail, take the Old Bruce Highway (Japoonvale Road) for 18.5km (11.5 miles) to **Paronella Park ❸** (Mena Creek; www.paronellapark.com.au; daily 9am–7.30pm; guided walks every 30 minutes 9.30am–4.30pm, night tour 6.15pm; charge). Back in 1913, Jose Paronella dreamt of building a Spanish castle alongside Mena Creek, and by 1935 his dream had been realised. A magnificent castle with grand staircase, lakeside tunnels and bridges, picnic areas and gardens was opened to the public. You can enjoy lunch at **Café on the Deck**, see ❶, overlooking Jose's eccentric creation.

MISSION BEACH

From Paronella Park, you are about 45 minutes from Mission Beach. Follow the signs south through Japoonvale to Silkwood on the Bruce Highway (23km/14 miles). Turn right onto the highway for **El Arish**, from where you turn left off the highway for the 16km (10-mile) drive to **Mission Beach ❹**. Made up of four communities – **Bingil Bay, Mission Beach** itself, **Wongaling Beach** and **South Mission Beach** – it has 14km (8.5 miles) of unspoilt coastline overlooking more than 20 offshore islands dotting the Coral Sea. The area offers a large array of activities, and you will find accommodation for all budgets (see page 109), including camping on Dunk Island (www.dunk-island.com).

Call in at the **Mission Beach Visitor Centre** (Porter Promenade; www.missionbeachtourism.com; Mon–Sat 9am–4.45pm, Sun 10am–4pm), located on the beachfront just outside Mission Beach village on the way to Bingil Bay. Here you'll find information on activities, galleries and accommodation options as well as details on the local mascot, the southern cassowary. Mission Beach is one of the few places where you're likely to see the this huge flightless bird.

Being the closest mainland point to the Great Barrier Reef, snorkelling and scuba-diving trips are popular and offer

White-water rafting

Near Tully, in a remote part of the Wet Tropics World Heritage Rainforest, the Tully River snakes through dramatic gorges. Its energy can be experienced on a full-day white-water rafting trip. Along its twisting, scenic descent there are over 45 churning (normally grade 3–4) rapids to conquer on a day packed with action and adventure. No prior experience is necessary, as river guides have intimate knowledge of every bend, curve and drop of the river and rapids. Trips with two main operators, RnR White Water Rafting Adventure (www.raft.com.au) and Raging Thunder (www.ragingthunder.com.au), are available year-round with transfers from/to your accommodation in Mission Beach, Cairns, Northern Beaches and Port Douglas. You need to be 13 years or older to raft.

White water rafting on the Tully River

a much quieter and less crowded option than those in Cairns. If you like your diving to be faster and less wet, try skydiving. Mission Beach is one of the most spectacular drop zones in the country. Check out Jump the Beach (www.jumpthebeach.com.au) for some serious thrills.

For a sleepy seaside town, Mission Beach has a surprising selection of good restaurants and eateries. **Miller's Beach Bar & Grill**, see ❷, offers a fantastic dining experience. **Dunk Island View Café**, see ❸, offers views of the island and wonderful fish and chips.

DUNK ISLAND

Offshore, the Family Group of Islands beckon. The most northerly, **Dunk Island** ❺, just 4km (2.5 miles) out to sea, was once a main attraction here, but Cyclone Yasi knocked the island around badly, and now it's only the real explorers that visit. The **water taxi** (Banfield Parade, Wongaling; www.missionbeachwatertaxi.com) still takes people to the island – a 10-minute crossing – three times a day (9am, 10am and 11am, returning 12pm and 3.30pm). Note that in order to board, you need to wade through shallow water. **Coral Sea Kayaking** (2 Wall Street, South Mission Beach; www.coralseakayaking.com) offer guided kayak trips to the island, including lunch and leisure time.

Dunk is a beautiful rainforested island offering 13km (8 miles) of walking tracks through most of the island's habitats and lovely secluded beaches.

Food and Drink

❶ CAFÉ ON THE DECK
Paronella Park, Japoonvale Road (Old Bruce Highway), Mena Creek; tel: 4065 0000; www.paronellapark.com.au; daily 9am–5pm; $
Enjoy a light lunch on the outdoor deck consisting of sandwiches, focaccias, pies or their celebrated homemade jam and scones.

❷ MILLERS BEACH BAR & GRILL
1 Banfield Parade, Wongaling Beach; tel: 4068 8177; www.millersbeachbar.com.au; Tue–Fri 3pm–late, Sat–Sun noon–late $
Almost universally acclaimed as the best place to eat around Mission Beach by locals and visitors alike, Millers is run by a couple of local food fans and combines friendly service with an awesome view, great drink deals and a killer menu. Try the oysters.

❸ DUNK ISLAND VIEW CAFÉ
21-35 Webb Road, Mission Beach; tel: 4068 8248; www.dunkislandviewcaravanpark.com/cafe; Tue–Wed 7.30am–4pm, Thur–Mon 7.30am–8pm; $
You might not be able to go and order a meal on Dunk Island at the moment, but you can enjoy some of the region's best fish and chips at this fantastic café with a view of the island. Also serves highly rated coffee.

DIRECTORY

Hand-picked hotels and restaurants to suit all budgets and tastes, organised by area, plus select nightlife listings, an alphabetical listing of practical information and an overview of the best books and films to give you a flavour of the city.

A room with a view at the Stamford Plaza

ACCOMMODATION

Coastal Queensland has a huge range of accommodation options, and you are unlikely to have any difficulty finding a place to stay unless there is a major event in progress when you plan to visit. Boutique rural retreats, hotels and hostels across inland areas, such as the Atherton Tablelands, are also becoming more popular, and self-catering cabins are always an interesting option to explore. When booking hotel accommodation, there is some latitude for striking a deal for longer stays, weekend rates, standby rates and so on. Check for internet-only rates, and it is always worth asking about 'specials' when speaking directly to the hotel. The vast majority of hotels have rooms for non-smokers, so request these when booking.

Brisbane

Banana Bender Backpackers
118 Petrie Terrace; tel: 3367 1157; www.bananabenders.com; $
Only a short bus ride from the city centre, this popular hostel has a range of room options, including female-only dorms and

Price for a double room for one night without breakfast:
$$$$ = over A$220
$$$ = A$150–220
$$ = A$80–150
$ = below A$80

double and twin rooms. The fan-cooled rooms are kept clean, and Bananas also offer airport shuttle service, internet access and backpacker party nights.

Brisbane City YHA
392 Upper Roma Street; tel: 3236 1004; www.yha.com.au; $
This convenient hostel – the winner of Best Backpacker Accommodation, Queensland Tourism Awards 2012 – is close to the Brisbane Transit Centre and to Caxton Street's fabulous nightlife. Rooms are either three-share or doubles, and all are air-conditioned. There's a good café, rooftop pool, games room full of electronic games, and a very helpful travel and tour desk.

Emporium Hotel
1000 Ann St, Fortitude Valley; tel: 3253 6999; www.emporiumhotels.com.au; $$$$
A Bohemian-flavoured luxury boutique hotel, with several design flourishes that leave an impression, including, in the Grand Onyx bar cocktail bar, an antique German chandelier originally from a castle in Europe. Rooms are equally as deluxe.

Lucerne on Fernberg
23 Fernberg Road, Paddington; tel: 3369 6686; www.lucerne.net.au; $$
A heritage-listed B&B in what is believed to be the oldest privately owned build-

Stamford Plaza Hotel is located by the Brisbane River

ing in Queensland. The beautifully presented accommodation is in the separate Coach House or Rose Cottage (the latter accessible for people in wheelchairs); both with mini home-theatre systems and cooking facilities. BBQ, parking and laundry facilities are available, and guests are welcome to enjoy the lovely wraparound veranda and gardens.

Pullman Brisbane King George Square

Corner of Ann and Roma streets;
tel: 3229 9111; www.accorhotels.com;
$$$$

Formerly the Sebel King George Square Hotel, the change in management here has seen a serious room revamp, striking a tidy balance between the needs of the holiday maker and the business guest - both of whom will appreciate the central location, views over King George Square and various luxury touches. Excellent facilities include parking, pool, restaurants and bar.

Rendezvous Studio Hotel on George

103 George Street; tel: 3221 6044;
www.rendezvoushotels.com/
brisbaneongeorge; $$$

Formerly the Marque, this modern boutique hotel is less than five minutes' walk from the city, casino or the river. It boasts excellent service and three grades of rooms, with the top-of-the-range spa suites overlooking the river and South Bank. Facilities include a heated outdoor pool, gymnasium, restaurant and bar, and undercover parking.

Rydges Southbank Hotel

9 Glenelg Streets, Southbank; tel: 3364 0800; www.rydges.com; $$$$

Location, location, location. Right near the South Bank Parklands and cultural precinct, with hundreds of rooms ranging over several categories, this five-star hotel can have great-value room deals on the internet. There are bars and restaurants, but you also have the great restaurants on Grey and Little Stanley streets nearby.

Spicers Balfour Hotel

37 Balfour Street, Brisbane; tel: 1300 597 540; www.spicersgroup.com.au; $$$$

With nine uniquely designed rooms, complemented by a communal library and a rooftop bar (serving sublime food) this European style boutique hotel is in New Farm, close to a wide variety of restaurants and overlooking the Brisbane River.

Stamford Plaza Hotel

Corner Margaret & Edward streets;
tel: 3221 1999; www.stamford.com.au;
$$$$

An elegant and contemporary hotel with a lovely heritage facade, located on the banks of the Brisbane River. All 252 rooms in the modern high-rise building boast panoramic river views and are comfortable and spacious.

Brisbane's river skyline is a sought-after view

Treasury Casino and Hotel

130 William Street; tel: 3306 8888;
www.treasurybrisbane.com.au; $$$$

An award-winning hotel located in the grand former Land Administration building, ideally situated in the heart of Brisbane with views of the river and South Bank across the street. Ornate and sumptuous heritage furnishings accentuate the hotel's opulent character, and the casino provides several dining and entertainment options.

Urban Hotel

345 Wickham Terrace; tel: 3831 6177;
http://hotelurban.com.au/brisbane; $$

Centrally located and surrounded by parklands, the boutique Urban has comfortable if simple rooms with small private balconies. The in-house Gazebo restaurant and bar offers relaxed dining with a 'fusion' menu – al fresco on the balcony, or inside – and the place has a touch of class. All guests have access to the Centenary Aquatic Centre.

Moreton Island

Blue Ocean View Beach House

Tangalooma, Moreton Island; tel: 0408 870 694; http://blueoceanviewbeachhouse. com; $$$

For fans of self-catering, this luxury beach house overlooking Moreton Bay and Tangalooma - the former whaling station where dolphins are now common visitors - is a slice of private luxury. With three bedrooms, two bathrooms and a deck, the house is spacious and fully kitted out, plus it's only a 60-minute ride on the Micat or Tangalooma Flyer from Brisbane. You even get to use the 6-seat electric golf buggy, for free.

Tangalooma Island Resort

tel: 3637 2000; www.tangalooma.com; $$$$

This efficient all-in-one, eco-friendly, family-focused resort offers numerous packages that include activities and tours such as the famous dolphin feeding at dusk. Choose between hotel rooms, serviced apartments, villa units and fully self-contained houses with various levels of comforts and luxury. There are several beachside restaurants for casual dining.

Sunshine Coast

10 Hastings Street Boutique Motel & Café

10 Hastings Street; tel: 5447 5800;
www.10hastingsstreet.com.au; $$

Formerly the Noosa Village Motel, this intimate venue has just undergone a A$1.5 million refurbishment, and is now looking the goods, with bright apartment suites and studios. The position, at the quieter end of Noosa's happening Hastings Street, close to Main Beach is perfect for both landscape leering and people watching. Great café too.

Breakfree French Quarter Resort

62 Hastings Street, Noosa Heads; tel: 5430 7100; www.frenchquarter.com.au; $$$

Right on Noosa's main drag and only 50m/yds from the beach, rooms here

Treasury Casino and Hotel　　　　　　　　　*An elegant Treasury hotel room*

are either one- or two-bedroom apart-ments with kitchenette and balcony overlooking Hastings Street with all its fine eateries, or the landscaped gardens with a lagoon-style pool.

Halse Lodge
2 Halse Lane, Noosa Heads; tel: 5447 3377; www.halselodge.com.au; $
This backpackers' retreat and YHA hos-tel is in a rambling old Queenslander surrounded by rainforest gardens with the surf beach only 100m/yds away. As well as dorms there are twin and double rooms and a restaurant and bar. Very popular, so book ahead.

North Stradbroke Island
Manta Lodge YHA
Point Lookout, North Stradbroke Island; 3409 8888; www.mantalodge.com.au; $
Perched right on the beachfront on gor-geous North Stradbroke Island, not only is this a super-friendly hostel offering superb value budget accommodation, it's also a 5-Star PADI dive resort offer-ing daily scuba dive and snorkel trips. Marine highlights here include manta rays encounters and shark dives with grey nurse sharks.

Stradbroke Island Beach Hotel and Spa Resort
East Coast Road, Point Lookout; tel: 3409 8188; www.stradbrokehotel.com. au; $$$
Situated atop a headland and overlook-ing pristine beaches where you may glimpse a whale, the 'Straddie Pub' offers luxury ocean-facing apartments plus hotel rooms and suites. Minimum stays of two or three nights apply, and a potential drawback – or plus – is that the popular bar and restaurant keep the action busy and the noise levels high until midnight.

Gold Coast
Coolangatta YHA
230 Coolangatta Road, Bilinga; tel: 5536 7644; www.coolangattayha. com; $
Only 500m/yds from Coolangatta Air-port and 150m/yds from the amazing surf of North Kirra Beach. Rooms range from dorms to singles, doubles and fam-ily rooms. Tour bookings, surfboard hire, surfing lessons and shuttles to the best breaks are all available. To say that this friendly hostel is surf-obsessed would be an understatement.

Hotel Grand Chancellor Surfers Paradise
Corner of Surfers Paradise Boulevard and Hanlan Street, Surfers Paradise; tel: 5579 3499; www.grandchancellorhotels.com/au/ surfersparadise; $$$
It's just 150 metres from the door of the hotel to the sand of Surfers here. Rooms have private balconies, so all you need to do is choose between an ocean and a city skyline view. Facilities include a pool and spa, and great sea-food is available at Hanlan's restaurant and bar.

Looking over Noosa's prime location

Hill Haven Holiday Apartments

2 Goodwin Terrace, Burleigh Heads; tel: 5535 1055; www.hillhaven.com.au; $$$

Nestled into the headland and adjoining Burleigh Heads National Park, this block of spacious apartments is superbly positioned with restaurants and a renowned surf beach just a short stroll away. Beautifully furnished two- and three-bedroom apartments offer panoramic views over Surfers Paradise, the ocean and the hinterland from balconies. The three-night booking minimum in the low season rises to five nights in the holiday season.

Oaks Calypso Plaza Resort

99 Griffith Street, Coolangatta; tel: 5599 0000; www.oakshotelsresorts.com/oaks-calypso-plaza; $$

An attractive, family-friendly, low-rise well away from the high-rise strip, very near the surf beach and airport. This well thought-out resort is equipped with a gym, games room and a lagoon-style swimming pool with waterslides. Rooms range from studios to one- and two-bedroom apartments. They regularly offer specials, so be sure to ask when you book.

Palazzo Versace

Sea World Drive, Main Beach; tel: 5509 8000; www.palazzoversace.com; $$$$

The ultimate in 'Renaissance' splendour, luxury and immaculate service is expressed in this 205-room hotel, the first venture into hotels by Donatella Versace. Supposedly a six-star establishment, it has all the style and extravagance associated with the brand liberally embossed throughout.

Pelican Cove

At Back and Burrows streets, Surfers Paradise; tel: 5537 7001; www.pelicancove.com.au; $$

This family-friendly resort has self-contained two- and three-bedroom units right on the Broadwater waterfront, with two saltwater swimming pools and spacious grounds. Just 10 minutes from Wet 'n' Wild, Dreamworld, Sea World and Movie World theme parks, and the tour desk sells discounted tickets.

Gold Coast hinterland

Binna Burra Mountain Lodge

Lamington National Park; tel: 5533 3622; www.binnaburralodge.com.au; $$$

Perched on a hinterland ridge with sweeping views, this award-winning eco-lodge is a romantic retreat, offering log cabins with dinner, bed and breakfast, or just bed-and-breakfast packages. There are also campsites available, plus a restaurant, spa and nature trails.

O'Reilly's Rainforest Retreat

Lamington National Park Road, via Canungra; tel: 5502 4911; www.oreillys.com.au; $$$$

The choice is simple here at this beautiful spot on the edge of the Lamington National Park: a mountain villas with all mod cons, including designer

A bright apartment at the Tangalooma Island Resort

decor, high-def LCD TV, rooms opening onto expansive private decks with outdoor spa bath and BBQ, or a complete digital detox in one of the Rainforest Retreats, which deliberately do not feature telephones or televisions, but which do boast king-size four-poster beds, en suite bathrooms and a couples' spa. The Canopy Suites also have open fireplaces. Minimum stay of two nights.

Fraser Island
Kingfisher Bay Resort
PMB 1 Urangan Hervey Bay; tel: 4194 9300; www.kingfisherbay.com; $$$$
A well-appointed eco-resort that has island-based hotel rooms, self-contained villas surrounded by rainforest, and multi-bedroom houses. The better rooms have sea views and spa baths. There are four swimming pools, four bars and four restaurants, and the resort has a helpful tour and activity desk.

Whitsunday Islands and Airlie Beach
Airlie Beach Hotel
At The Esplanade and Coconut Grove, Airlie Beach; tel: 4964 1999; www.airliebeach hotel.com.au; $$–$$$$
A prime seafront location with four-star facilities makes this one of the busier hotels in town, but justifiably so. Hotel rooms have either beach-view or town-view balconies and sleep either two or three people. Less expensive, three-star motel rooms do not have the balcony views. There are three restaurants on site, and the main drag is only a stroll away.

Coral Sea Resort
25 Oceanview Avenue, Airlie Beach; tel: 4964 1300; www.coralsearesort.com; $$$
The only absolute waterfront resort in Airlie Beach offers a range of apartment-style rooms, many with spa baths, near the Abel Point marina. The resort is just three minutes' stroll along a boardwalk from Airlie Beach's main drag. The setting is stunning, with a large pool, great patio café and bar, and the resort's own jetty doubles as a dining venue. The rooms range from one-bedroom hotel rooms to suites, apartments and penthouses.

Hamilton Island
Tel: 4946 9999; www.hamiltonisland.com. au; $$$$
A range of room types are available on this highly developed, self-contained island – and all of them are expensive. Choose from the exclusive Qualia, Beach Club, Reef View Hotel and the Palm Bungalows. The latter is the cheapest option, while Qualia occupies the other end of the spectrum. There's a staggering range of recreation and dining options, too.

Magnums Backpackers
366 Shute Harbour Road, Airlie Beach; tel: 4964 1199; www.magnums.com.au; $

The most central hostel at Airlie is also one of the friendliest. It offers dormitory, twin share and double accommodation, and the cheapest beer in town. There's a helpful tour desk, and it is right across the road from the swimming lagoon.

Reef Sleep

ReefWorld, Great Barrier Reef, off Hamilton Island; tel: 4946 4662; www.cruise whitsundays.com/gbra-Reefsleep.aspx; $$$$

Slumber under the stars on the roof of a pontoon in the midst of the Great Barrier Reef, being rocked to sleep by the gentle movement of the Coral Sea while you snuggle into the most Australian of all inventions: the swag (a cross between a sleeping bag and a tent). This is a new offering from Cruise Whitsundays, and besides an al fresco sleeping experience you'll also enjoy 5-star hospitality (meals served in an underwater chamber looking out on the reef) and a chance to go night diving before you turn in for the night.

Cairns

Acacia Court Hotel

223–227 The Esplanade; tel: 4051 5011; www.acaciacourt.com: $$

The Acacia Court Hotel is just 2km (1.25 miles) from the city centre, a pleasant walk along The Esplanade. Rooms have queen-size beds, en suite bath or shower rooms, and balconies with either ocean or mountain views. There are also cheaper motel-style rooms. The on-site restaurant Charlie's has an all-you-can-eat buffet every night.

Cairns Central YHA

20-26 McLeod Street; tel: 4051 0772; www3.yha.com.au; $

A large and buzzing youth hostel, complete with a welcoming swimming pool to dive into when the tropical heat gets a little too much to bear. The YHA is centrally located and has plenty of communal facilities, including internet facilities and a laundry. Get up early and you can blag yourself a share of the free pancakes that are cooked and handed out each morning. Family rooms are also available.

Galvins Edge Hill B&B

61 Walsh Street; tel: 4032 1308; www.galvinsonedge.com.au; $$$

This welcoming B&B is in a genuine old Queenslander in a peaceful location. With a lounge and breakfast room that opens onto the natural-rock swimming pool, and just two bedrooms and a bathroom, only one family or group is booked at a time, so you have the whole place to yourselves.

Gilligan's Backpackers Hotel and Resort

57–89 Grafton Street; tel: 4041 6566; www.gilligansbackpackers.com.au; $

This huge and often raucous backpackers' resort offers economical dorm beds plus twin and double rooms, rowdy entertainment and a social soup of a

High-rises frame Main Beach on the Gold Coast

swimming pool. All rooms are air-conditioned and have en suite bathrooms, and each floor has its own kitchen. Guests get free airport transfers.

Shangri-La Hotel
The Marina, Pier Point Road; tel: 4031 1411; www.shangri-la.com/cairns; $$$$
Fronting the turquoise waters of Trinity Inlet and the Marlin Marina with its bobbing luxury flotilla, this luxury hotel has excellent views and a convenient location. Rooms and suites boast private balconies or patios and a range of leisure facilities, including a large swimming pool, in more than an acre of lush tropical gardens.

Palm Cove

Hotel Grand Chancellor Palm Cove
Coral Coast Drive, Palm Cove; tel: 4059 1234; www.grandchancellorhotels.com/au/palmcove; $$
Perfect for travelling families, this resort has a games room and not one but two swimming pools, one boasting watersides and other small-person crowd pleasing features. For bigger guests there's a bar, alfresco dining area and various pampering facilities. It's only 5 minutes' walk to the beach.

The Reef Retreat
10–14 Harpa Street Palm Cove; tel: 4059 1744; www.reefretreat.com.au; $$
Just across from the beach at Palm Cove, Reef Retreat offers a lovely low-rise alternative to those who don't want the big hotel experience. Accommodation is in a collection of self-contained boutique apartments set in a verdant rainforest setting, complete with refreshing pool, a spa and communal BBQs. Owners couldn't be more friendly and welcoming.

Sebel Reef House & Spa
99 Williams Esplanade; tel: 4080 2600; www.reefhouse.com.au; $$$$
Much-heralded boutique property just opposite the beach at Palm Cove. Its bygone-era Queensland architecture is truly charming, with 69 oversized rooms and suites accented by wooden shutters, terracotta floors, wicker furniture and mosquito nets draped over beds. Lush gardens, a courtyard pool and a delightful restaurant complete the picture.

Port Douglas

Hibiscus Gardens Spa Resort
22 Owens Street; tel: 4099 5315; www.hibiscusportdouglas.com.au; $$$
Set among exotic gardens with two pools, this neat hotel has a Balinese theme. Accommodation spans motel-style to three-bedroom apartments, some with private spas. And it is less than five minutes' walk to the beach and shops.

Rendezvous Reef Resort
121 Port Douglas Road; tel 4087 2790; www.rendezvoushotels.com/portdouglas; $$

Palazzo Versace's opulent style

Sprawling cross 15 acres of lush tropical gardens, this resort is one for water babies, boasting two lagoon-style pools, one leisure pool, one 25-metre lap pool (with eight lanes) and one children's pool - and of course the beach is only across the road. A short stroll out of town, the Port Douglas Shuttle runs every 15 minutes will give you a ride if it's too hot to walk. Rooms are modern and clean, many are split level with balconies overlooking the pools.

Sheraton Mirage Port Douglas Resort

Port Douglas Road; tel: 4099 5888; www.sheratonportdouglas.com; $$$$
Almost 300 rooms and over 100 villas circle an epic swimming lagoon in this sprawling 130-hectare resort, a stretch of luxurious greenery that spoons Four Mile Beach for several hundred metres. You can access the beach from the resort, perfect for sunrise and sunset wanders along the sand into town. The bar and restaurant are under cover, but with views out across the property.

Daintree and Cape Tribulation

Cape Tribulation Beach House Resort

152 Rykers Road, Cape Tribulation; tel: 4098 0030; www.capetribbeach.com.au; $-$$$
Situated 48km (30 miles) from the ferry terminal, this place provides dormitory and family cabins across eight price categories to cater for all budgets. Common areas include the saltwater swimming pool, the Sand Bar and Bistro, and communal kitchen and laundry facilities for self-caterers. It is located as close to the beach as the National Parks Authority will allow.

Daintree Eco Lodge & Spa

20 Daintree Road, Daintree; tel: 4098 6100; www.daintree-ecolodge.com.au; $$$$
Just 15 private cabins are offered at this luxurious nature retreat nestled into the rainforest a short drive from Daintree village. It's not one for families, but a great romantic splurge with a well-being spa and restaurant that takes cues from the local environment and indigenous knowledge to create its Australian tropical cuisine.

Ferntree Rainforest Lodge

36 Camelot Close, Cape Tribulation; tel: 4098 0000; www.ferntreerainforestlodge.com.au; $$
There's a large selection of accommodation options here, ranging from budget dorm rooms right through to split-level cabins set in the rainforest garden, poolside suites with balconies looking over a lagoon, and secluded private cabins. The Cassowary Café serves a good selection of food daily and the owners can also help arrange tours.

Atherton Tablelands

Barking Owl Retreat

409 Hough Road, Kairi, Atherton

Cairns' Shangri-La Hotel

Tablelands; tel: 4095 8455; www.barkingowl retreat.com.au; $$$

Stay a night or two in the so-much-friendlier-than-it-sounds 'Dingo's Lair', and experience the Atherton Tablelands as they should be seen, from a verandah with only the sounds of the bush to interrupt your reverie. The property boasts a dam where you can fish (and release), or sit chatting around the firepit, and your hosts are friendly and knowledgeable.

Cedar Park Rainforest Resort

250 Cedarpark Road, Kuranda; tel: 4093 7892; www.cedarparkresort.com.au; $$

Somewhere between Kuranda and Mareeba, up on the Atherton Tablelands, you'll find this spellbinding place. With just five rooms, set in an idyllic rainforest environment full of wildlife, it's run by super-friendly Swiss ex-pats, who will spoil you rotten. The layout of the place is eccentric, which adds to the charm, and among its many great features is an al fresco restaurant overlooking the Wet Tropics World Heritage Rainforest. Dinner is served every night, whenever you want it.

Eden House Retreat and Mountain Spa

20 Gillies Highway, Yungaburra; tel: 4089 7000; www.edenhouse.com.au; $$$

This exquisite heritage retreat offers secluded cottages and villas with private spas set in luxuriant gardens. Although aimed at couples looking for a relaxing escape (four-poster safari-style beds included), there is adequate accommodation for families as well. There's a restaurant and bar and the excellent Mountain Spa that offers a wide range of indulgent packages to pamper your body and soul.

Mission Beach

The Elandra at Mission Beach

Explorer Drive, South Mission Beach; tel: 4068 8154; www.elandraresorts.com; $$$–$$$$

The views from this resort-style hotel, on the southern headland above Mission Beach, are magnificent. The luxury accommodation with its chic African tribal theme is set amidst rainforest rich in wildlife, and the building is architecturally designed so that everybody enjoys privacy and an elevated ocean and beach view.

Sejala on the Beach

Mission Beach; 0455 898 699; www.sejala. com.au/beach-house; $$$$

Choose between three beautiful boutique beachfront huts (en-suite and complete with air-con and beachfront verandahs), tucked away in a tropical garden and just metres away from one of the world's best beaches, or the big, spacious beach house. Facilities to tempt you out of your hammock include a private in-house glass tiled terrace pool set amid pink ginger, mandevillea and lime trees.

RESTAURANTS

In Brisbane and Cairns and along the coast where tourism is significant, you will have no trouble finding quality fresh food prepared with flair – and usually with multicultural influences. In Brisbane, there are several restaurant neighbourhoods just a few minutes' cab drive or bus/ferry ride from the CBD (see page 15), while in Cairns, Shields Street is known as 'Eats Street', with more dining options along the boardwalk facing the Marlin Marina and along the Esplanade. On the islands around the reef, the fact that resort-based restaurants basically have you at their mercy can sometimes mean that prices are high, but the quality should also be top notch – their reputation as a destination depends on it.

The foundation of Australian cuisine is the quality and variety of its ingredients. Locally sourced produce, meats and fish are highly sought after. Aussies were slow to recognise the wealth of seafood in their waters, but now a range of fresh fish is on every menu. Small farms devote themselves to gourmet beef and poultry, while the qual-

ity of everyday vegetables rivals that grown on organic farms in Europe or the United States. Far from pining for imports of French cheese, Greek olives or Italian wine, Australians produce their own, which are often rated superior to the imports.

Australia can be divided into regions that are known for particular produce and each state has its acknowledged specialities. In the case of tropical Queensland, they are the wealth of exotic fruits, like Bowen mangoes and papaya, as well as succulent reef fish, mudcrabs and Moreton Bay Bugs (see page 14).

Brisbane

Alchemy Restaurant and Bar

175 Eagle Street; tel: 3229 3175; www.alchemyrestaurant.com.au; Mon–Fri 12–3pm, 6–10pm; Sat 6pm–late; $$$

A Brisbane favourite for many years, the Alchemy's beef cheeks are legendary, but the European-flavoured menu is eclectic and sophisticated, and includes a wonderful cheese list. The location, right by the Brisbane River overlooking the Story Bridge, just adds spice to the experience.

Aria Restaurant

Eagle Street Pier, Eagle Street; tel: 3233 2555; www.ariarestaurant.com/brisbane; Mon–Fri noon–2.30pm, 5.30–10.30pm, Sat

> Price range for a two-course meal for one including a glass of house wine:
> $$$=over A$60
> $$=A$40–60
> $=below $40

The dining room at Aria

5–10.30pm, Sun 5.30–9.30pm; $$$
Also with spectacular views over Story Bridge and the Brisbane River, Aria has an elegant contemporary menu devised by celebrity chef Matt Moran. Seafood and top-quality steaks dominate, but there are vegetarian options and delicate Asian interpretations. The innovative cuisine is matched to an extensive wine list, showcasing many of Australia's iconic wineries.

Augustine's on George

40 George Street; tel: 3229 0014; www.augustines.com.au; Mon–Fri noon–2.30pm & 6–10pm, Sat 6–10pm; $$$
Hong Kong expatriate Augustine Tso has been a flag on Brisbane's fine-dining map for more than 25 years. The quality at this snug restaurant has never wavered: thoughtful, flavoursome dishes that sit lightly on the palate. Entrées such as soufflé gruyère and truffle with baby salad and toasted hazelnuts set the scene for mains like barramundi fillet with citrus and herb crust, king prawns and beurre blanc.

Baguette Bistro & Bar

150 Racecourse Road; tel: 3268 6168; www.baguette.com.au; Sat–Sun 9am–2pm, Mon–Fri 11.30am–3pm, Mon–Sat 5.30pm–late, Sat–Sun; $$$
Brett's Wharf may be gone – much to the distress of seafood lovers all over the city, but restaurateurs Francis and Marilyn Domenech are still going strong with this, Brisbane's oldest French restaurant, which manages to mix Gallic flair with Queensland fair in terms of both cuisine and culture. Try the Classic Bistro Lyonnaise (quenelles with shellfish sauce and grilled tiger prawns)

Breakfast Creek Hotel

2 Kingsford Smith Drive, Albion; tel: 3262 5988; www.breakfast creekhotel.com; daily noon–2.30pm, 6–10.30pm; $$
The Brekkie's steaks are virtually the size of a dinner plate, and consistently thick, juicy and flavoursome. Choose your own from 12 premium cuts at the barbecue in the Beer Garden or visit the Spanish Garden Steakhouse for full table service and other menu items. But it's the steaks that make this place famous.

Cha Cha Char Wine Bar and Grill

Shop 5 Plaza Level, Eagle Street Pier; tel: 3211 9944; www.chachachar.com.au; Mon–Fri noon–11pm, Sat–Sun 6–11pm; $$$
If you still have not succumbed to Queensland's obsession with succulent steaks, here is the place to give in to temptation. The menu will make you an instant expert in all things steaky. Digest the facts about breeding, feed, location and age before devouring the subject. Booking is recommended.

Crosstown Eating House

23 Logan Road, Woolloongabba; tel: 3162 3839; www.thecrosstown.com.au;

E'cco restaurant in Brisbane

Tue 6pm–9.30pm, Wed–Sat 7am-2.30pm, noon–9.45pm; $

Nestled in a two-storey brick house on Logan Road, the Crosstown has been getting plenty of traffic recently, thanks to its welcoming culture. non pretentious attitude – 'a boisterous eating house and bar that serves lunch and dinner in a casual and friendly environment' – and quality menu. Have a crack at the Kinkawooka mussels with fries, or sink your teeth into a plate of pan-fried Tasmanian salmon.

E'cco

100 Boundary Street (corner with Adelaide Street East); tel: 3831 8344; www.eccobistro.com; Tue–Fri noon–2.30pm, 6pm–late, Sat 6pm–late; $$$

A multi-award winning bistro, thanks to Philip Johnson's simple philosophy: 'Real food, honest food, using the best local produce'. Settle in for field mushrooms, olive toast, rocket and parmesan, or try rare-seared Wagyu beef salad with Asian herbs, chilli caramel and candied sesame seeds. And that's just for starters. Mains on an ever-evolving menu currently include offerings such as roast duck breast, pear, sour cherry and pine nut tarte tatin.

Gambaro's Seafood Restaurant

33 Caxton Street, Petrie Terrace, Paddington; tel: 3369 9500; www.gambaros.com.au; Mon–Fri noon–2pm & 6pm–late, Sat 5pm–late; $$$

The Gambaro family have been in the seafood business since 1953, and Gambaro's has been a Brisbane institution since it opened in 1972. The seafood platters are a gastronomic delight, and from the tanks you can select Moreton Bay bugs, lobster and mud crabs. While seafood is what the restaurant specialises in, there are other options, including steak, chicken and pasta dishes.

Gerard's Bistro

Shop 14, 15 James Street Fortitude Valley; tel: 3852 3822; www.gerardsbistro.com.au; breakfast, lunch and dinner; $$

Since opening in July 2012, this James Street venue has been getting tongues flapping and stomachs rumbling. Head Chef, Ben Williamson, has a solid reputation base don past glories (at Cha Cha Char and Urbane) and in his creations you can taste influences from all around the Mediterranean, Northern Africa, and the Middle East. Try the pigeon breast with beetroot and raspberries or the Boer goat tagine.

Green Papaya

898 Stanley Street (corner with Potts Street), East Brisbane; tel: 3891 5000; www.greenpapaya.com.au; Fri noon–2.30pm and 5.30–9.30pm, Tue–Thur and Sat–Sun 5.30–9.30pm; $$$

Former chef, Lien Yeomans, has gone, and with her departure Green Papaya has switched from offering the North Vietnamese cuisine that initially got

Aria's fine seafood

people talking, to serving up the best Balinese and Thai food in town. Try the double-cooked pork belly or the pad prik gaeng soft shell crab. If you like what they do (and you will) ask about their cooking school.

Hatch and Co

Gasworks Plaza; tel: 3257 2969; www.hatchandco.com.au; daily 12pm–late; $$$

Braden White, the man in charge of the knives at this chilled out venue in Newstead's stylish Gasworks Plaza, is a highly rated young chef. Despite his tender age, he is a disciple of traditional slow cooking techniques, and utilises local and sustainable produce to turn out hearty fare including flavoursome pizzas and generous share plates – try the pork cheek or the barramundi with crispy artichoke. The cheerful restaurant has a bar alfresco dining area.

Il Centro Restaurant

Eagle Street Pier, Eagle Street; tel: 3221 6090; www.il-centro.com.au; Sun–Fri noon–2.30pm and 5.30pm–late, Sat 5.30pm–late; $$$

Il Centro is one of a trio of quality restaurants overlooking the Brisbane River at the Eagle Street Pier complex. Executive chef Catherine Anders marries Italian recipes with Queensland produce with flair. Expect wonderful seafood and pasta – try the celebrated lasagne *alla granseola* (sand crab lasagne) – plus prime cuts of steak.

Jade Buddha

Eagle Street Pier, Eagle Street; tel: 3221 2888; www.jadebuddha.com.au; daily 11.30am–late; $$$

With its Asian-fusion cuisine using plenty of fresh seafood, plus colourful cocktails in the trendy Shadow Lounge, the 'Buddha' attracts Brisbane's glitterati. There are plenty of moreish bar snacks and light meals to kick the night off while feasting on excellent river and bridge views. Try the seafood laksa, chicken katsu curry or the Balinese-style lamb.

Moda Restaurant

12 Edward Street; tel: 3221 7655; www.modarestaurant.com.au; Mon–Sat from 6pm, Thur–Fri from noon; $$

By blending lovely local ingredients with intriguing ideas from his native Catalonia, chef Javier Codina creates something special in this venue, which is famous for its Pica Pica lunches (an eclectic mix of five Spanish inspired dishes plus café con dulces) and paella Fridays. At other times get stuck into quality French Italian and Catalan cuisine, with tasty plates such as lamb adobo and ocean trout balloting with goat's curd and salmon caviar.

Obsession Restaurant

5 Little Stanley Street; tel: 3844 3373; www.obsessionchinese.com.au; Mon

Brisbane's climate is conducive to outdoor dining

11am–3pm, Sun–Thur 11am–3pm & 5–10pm, Fri–Sat 11am–3pm & 5–11pm; $$$

Delicate Chinese and Southeast Asian specialities, such as Singapore-style chilli bugs and *ma po* tofu, are prepared with organic and free-range produce in a chic setting with indoor and pavement seating.

Riverbar and Kitchen

Riparian Plaza, Promenade Level, 71 Eagle Street; tel: 3211 9020; www.riverbarandkitchen.com.au; Mon–Fri 7am–11.30pm, Sat–Sun 8am–11.30pm; $

Drop in (you can't book), order at the bar, sit back and drink in the views of the Story Bridge while sipping a quality coffee, and wait for the goodness to arrive in this bright and relaxed riverside joint. Breakfasts to see you right through the day include baked eggs, black pudding, spicy tomato, spinach and flatbread, while later on crack open a bottle of King Valley Pinot Grigio and tuck into a plate of chili salt squid with coriander and lime.

Spring Food & Wine

26 Felix Street; tel: 3229 0460; www.spring.com.au; Mon–Fri 7am–late, Sat 8am–late; $$

Spring's menu is entirely comprised of seasonal produce, carefully matched to a list of wines sourced from artisanal vintners. Open from 7am, they serve breakfast, brunch, lunch, dinner, dessert and high tea, and then there's a tuck shop menu in case you get peckish in between. For lunch you can try Crumbed Hinterland zucchini flowers with feta, gin gin smoked tomatoes, and for dinner Dakota Vale roast chicken with green beans and almonds. There's a cooking school too.

Tank Bar

North Quarter Lane, 32 Turbot Street; tel: 3003 1993, Mon–Fri- 11am–late, Sat–Sun closed; $$

Executive chef Tyrone Bramley uses lessons learnt on his travels throughout Southeast Asia, North America and Europe to fuse international influences with Australian ingredients to excellent effect at this weekday only laneway venue. Try the market fish with lemongrass mash, wild harvest mushroom risotto with asparagus and hazelnuts, or the sand crab linguine.

Sunshine Coast

Bistro C

49 Hastings Street, Noosa Heads; tel: 5447 2855; www.bistroc.com.au; daily 7.30am–10pm; $$$

This chic beachside restaurant epitomises the modern Australian dining scene, with an imaginative menu fusing the tastes of the Mediterranean and Asia with Australia's bounty of fresh ingredients. There are five separate, regularly changing menus throughout the day, which offer a wide-ranging selection from coconut chicken salad to caramelised pork belly.

A streetside seat   *Moreton Bay Bugs in a seafood platter*

Gold Coast

Absynthe

Q1 complex, 9 Hamilton Avenue, Surfers
Paradise; tel: 5504 6466; www.absynthe.
com.au; Fri noon–2pm and 6–9.30pm,
Mon–Sat 6–9.30pm; $$$

Celebrated French chef Meyjitte
Boughenout lends a dash of Gallic
élan to the 80-storey Q1 building. His
restaurant is famous for juxtaposing
the most unlikely of flavours to create
taste sensations that are as beguiling
as they are unexpected. Ingredients
include Périgord truffle, royal cav-
iar and gold leaf accompanying fresh
ingredients such as ocean trout, rab-
bit and duck sourced from all over
Australia.

The Broadbeach Tavern

Oasis Shopping Centre, Old Burleigh
Road, Broadbeach; tel: 5538 4111;
www.broadbeachtavern.com.au; daily
11.30am–2.30pm and 5.30–8.30pm; $

Choose simple, good-quality meals
from a small and inexpensive menu
including items such as burgers, fish
and chips, and juicy steaks. The tavern
is an unpretentious place where guest
bands enliven the atmosphere most
nights and live sport is splashed across
screens throughout.

Oskars on Burleigh

Burleigh Beach House, 43 Goodwin
Terrace, Burleigh Heads; tel: 5576 3722;
www.oskars.com.au; daily noon–2.30pm,
6–10pm; $$$

Oskars has been a Gold Coast institution for 28 years, and it is easy to see
why. Owner Kieran Daly personally
selects the seafood-dominated menu,
which changes daily, but the twice-
baked sand crab soufflé with tomato
compote, rocket and walnut salad is a
frequent entrée. The beach location,
with sweeping ocean views north to
Surfers Paradise, is a strong component
of its appeal.

Ristorante Fellini

Marina Mirage, Seaworld Drive, Main
Beach; tel: 5531 0300; www.fellini.com.au;
daily noon–2.30pm, 6–10pm; $$–$$$

Brothers Carlo and Tony Percuoco dish
up superb Italian cuisine within their
elegant, award-winning restaurant. Try
the pasta *linguette allo zafferano* – saf-
fron-infused long flat pasta cooked with
Moreton Bay bug meat in a light cream
sauce. Like other creations on the
menu, the dish makes a virtue of sim-
plicity, and is a perennial favourite with
regulars. The restaurant looks across
the Southport Broadwater, and behind
it stands the Percuoco's pasta shop,
Pastificio Fellini, where the available
lines include ravioli filled with crabmeat
and leek cooked in Sauvignon blanc.

Seaduction Restaurant + Bar

Level 2, Soul Surfers Paradise, 8
The Esplanade; tel: 5635 5728;
www.seaduction.com.au; daily 6.30am–
10.30am, Tue–Sun 12–2.30pm, Tue–Sat
6.30–9.30pm; $$$

Modern styling at Absynthe

Killer views out over the ocean waves, but don't be fooled by the name, there's more to this joint than seafood – in fact, the menu has an Italian accent to it, and the duck is their signature dish.

Shuck

20 Tedder Avenue, Main Beach; tel: 5528 4286; www.shuck.com.au; daily noon–late; $$$

As the name implies, Shuck is noted for oysters, along with excellent seafood chowder, bouillabaisse, crab lasagne and... the ubiquitous steaks. Seating is mainly alfresco, with courtyard tables overlooking a passing parade of poseurs. The Mod Oz cuisine, open-air setting and general relaxed vibe make it exactly right for this trendy Gold Coast precinct.

Gold Coast hinterland

St Bernards Hotel

101 Alpine Terrace, Mount Tamborine; tel: 5545 1177; www.stbernardshotel.com; noon–2pm, 6–8pm; $$

Venerable St Bernards has the ambience of a country pub far removed from the chintzy fudge shops and galleries that dominate the mountain. Enjoy hearty pub food, such as salt-and-pepper calamari and eye fillet steak, served with just enough flair to keep it interesting.

Binna Burra Mountain lodge

Binna Burra Mountain Lodge, Lamington National Park; tel: 5533 3622; www.binnaburralodge.com.au; daily, hours below; $$

Enjoy the sweeping ridge-top views over the rainforest, Numbah Valley and the coast, while choosing from a casual lunch and tea menu, including burgers, salads and scones in the Lamington Tea House (Mon–Thur 10am–3pm, Fri 10am–8pm, Sat 7.30am–8pm, Sun 7.30am–4.30pm). Hearty breakfasts and dinners are served up in the Clifftop Dining Room (breakfast 7.30am–9.30am, bar from 3pm, dinner from 6.30pm).

Fraser Island

Seabelle Restaurant

Kingfisher Bay Resort, Fraser Island; tel: 4120 3333; www.kingfisherbay.com; daily 6.30–10pm; $$$

Describing its food as a bush-tucker dining experience, Seabelle Restaurant offers dishes that are inspired by ingredients traditionally used by indigenous people. Try the K'gari signature plate of chargrilled crocodile, kangaroo and emu with bunya nut pesto, bush tomato chutney, rosella and chilli plum jam, with a lemon myrtle panna cotta for dessert.

Airlie Beach

Capers at the Beach

Airlie Beach Hotel, The Esplanade, Airlie Beach; tel: 4964 1999; www.airlie beachhotel.com.au; daily 7am–11am, noon–2.30pm, 6–9.30pm, until 10pm Fri–Sat; $$$

Much 'Mod Oz' fare focusses on seafood

Capers is a lively beachsiderestaurant offering a modern Australian menu of local seafood and sumptuous steaks. Their 'Localvore' menu uses ingredients sourced solely within 100km (60 miles) of the restaurant.

Cairns

Bayleaf
Corner of Lake and Gatton Streets; tel: 40514622; www.bayvillage.com.au; daily 6.30–9.30am, Mon–Fri noon–2pm, nightly 6pm–late

As the old adage says, go where the locals go, and Cairns people flock to this Balinese Restaurant in the Bay Village Tropical Retrat, and then rave about it – and deservedly so. The chefs here are all graduates of the highly regarded Bumbu Bali Restaurant and Cooking School in Bali. The pork dishes are something truly special. There's a selection of around five curries, most involving fall-apart tender meat. Also open for breakfast.

Café China
Rydges Plaza Complex, corner of Spence and Grafton Streets; tel: 4041 2828; www.cafechina.com.au; daily 11am–late; $$

Try delicious mainly Beijing and Hong Kong dishes, with some Szechuan menu entries, dim sum, seafood and noodles cooked in a healthy low-fat style with no added MSG. House specialties include salt-and-pepper mud crab, Peking duck and steamed coral trout. Owner Harry Sou makes sure that diners are well looked after.

Donnini's
34 Esplanade (at the Hilton); tel: 4051 1133; www.donniniscairns.com.au; daily 11am–late; $$

In a new home, having swapped the Marina for the Hilton on the Esplanade, the quality and value offered by this excellent and authentic Italian restaurant hasn't changed – although it has reverted back to it original owner. Pizza and pasta dishes reign supreme, with highlights listed on the daily specials board. The service is helpful and friendly.

Fusion
2/135 Grafton Street (Corner with Alpin Street); tel 4051 1388; www.fusionorganics.com.au; Mon–Fri 7am–3pm, Sat 7am–2pm; $

A funky fusion joint in the heart of Cairns, which caters for those who like their produce fresh and organic. A beacon of light for vegans and veggies in this meat-obsessed country (although committed carnivores can still munch chicken and tuna). Try the gluten-free pasta or an egg-less vegetable terrine – even dairy lovers will be pleasantly surprised. Juices and smoothies rule the roost here, but the coffee is damn good too.

Khin Kao Thai Restaurant
At Aplin and Grafton Streets; tel: 4031

8581; www.khinkhao.com.au; daily 11am–2pm, 5.30–10pm; $$
The best Thai restaurant in Cairns is a popular venue indeed with an extensive menu of all the favourites – such as Massaman, yellow, green and red curries – making full and fantastic use of the local seafood. Service is efficient and the prices are very reasonable, including a good-value daily lunch special.

Ochre Restaurant

43 Shields Street; tel: 4051 0100; www.ochrerestaurant.com.au; Mon–Fri noon–2.30pm & 6–10pm, Sat–Sun 6–10pm; $$$
In this multi-award-winning restaurant, creative modern Australian cuisine is offered with inventive flair that uses 40 different native ingredients to enhance dishes based on kangaroo, crocodile, beef, tropical fruit and local seafood. Try the kangaroo sirloin with *quandong* chilli glaze, and for dessert, wattleseed pavlova with Davidson plum sorbet, or check the daily specials board.

Salt House Marina Point

6/2 Pier Point Road; tel: 4041 7733; www.salthouse.com.au; Mon–Thur noon–midnight, Fri–Sat 7am–2am, Sun 7am–midnight; $$
The modern design of this large, open-plan restaurant makes the most of its prime waterfront position looking out on the Coral Sea. Great for breakfast (at weekends), lunch, or afternoon tapas, it really comes into its own at dinner when steaks and seafood are seared on the immense wood-fired grill. There's live music, and the scene can start pumping at night, particularly towards the end of the week. This is an all-night venue, with an outdoor cocktail bar surrounded by water and fire features, and a glowing bar at the front where bands play four nights a week.

Tamarind

Reef Casino, 35-41 Wharf Street; tel: 4030 8888; Tue–Sat 6–10:30pm
Set in the Reef Casino, this award-winning Asian fusion restaurant is helmed by chef Mark Jensen. The fine dining on offer makes the most of regional ingredients, paired with an extensive wine list and a range of cocktails. There is a daily degustation menu available.

Port Douglas

Nautilus Restaurant

17 Murphy Street; tel: 4099 5330; www.nautilus-restaurant.com.au; daily 6.30pm–midnight; $$$
Everybody in Port Douglas goes to the Nautilus at least once. All the celebrities have been – along with thousands of others who soak up the tropical ambience of a unique outdoor dining experience while enjoying the top-flight dinner menu.

Salsa Bar and Grill

26 Wharf Street; tel: 4099 4922; www.salsaportdouglas.com.au;

A prime table at Oskars on Burleigh

daily noon–midnight; $$$
Head chef Goran Zonai puts all his expertise and his multi-national team to excellent use here, delivering a menu that explodes with flavour and creativity. Salsa has won multiple awards, and the walls of the restaurant are covered in plates signed by visiting celebrities, including one autographed by Bill Clinton (check out the date on the plate – it'll give you goose bumps). Tough choice between the linguini pepperincino with tableland red claw, and the kangaroo fillet, but the dessert is a no brainer: go the decadent tasting plate for two.

The Wharf Street Bistro

Court House Hotel, Corner Wharf and Macrossan Streets, Port Douglas; tel: 4099 5181; www.courthousehotelportdouglas. com.au; daily 11.30am–9.30pm; $$
Renowned for having the best steaks in town, so order your favourite cut from the grill. Other temptations from the extensive menu include BBQ pork spare ribs and the Coral Sea curry, a Thai-style seafood curry. This pub has atmosphere, entertainment and clientele spilling out onto the pavement and balconies.

Zinc

3 / 53-61 Macrossan Street; tel: 4099 6260; www.zincportdouglas.com; daily 10am–late; $$$
A long-standing Port favourite, known locally as The Tin Shed, this edge-of-the-port restaurant specialises in local seafood, serving fantastic dishes with prawns, bugs, Barramundi and other locally-caught fish. Their poultry and meat offering is impressive too though – try the Mandarin-glazed twice-cooked duck leg. Time your visit to coincide with high tide, when the view is awesome – even from the toilet.

Daintree

Julaymba Restaurant and Gallery

Daintree Eco Lodge and Spa, 20 Daintree Road, Daintree; tel: 1800 808 010; www.daintree-ecolodge.com.au; daily 8am–10am, noon–2pm, dinner from 6.30pm; $$$
This serene restaurant, held in the arms of the ancient rainforest and overlooking a freshwater lagoon infuses indigenous fruits, nuts and berries with fine-dining. Try the seafood tapas, wok-tossed fresh king prawns, or the macadamia- and herb-crusted lamb fillet.

Mission Beach

Elandra Restaurant and Bar

Explorer Drive, South Mission Beach; tel: 4068 8154; www.elandraresorts.com; daily 7am–9pm; $$$
Sitting high on a cliff edge where rainforest meets the sea, enjoy modern Australian cuisine with an Asian influence, such as seared king scallops, drunken chicken or a warm Asian noodle salad. Even if you do not feel like eating, you can feast your eyes on the collection of tribal arts and artefacts from across the globe.

NIGHTLIFE

Don't go looking for wall-to-wall sophistication in Queensland, particularly in the north. Nightlife in Cairns, Airlie Beach and Mission Beach focuses largely on the backpacker party circuit, featuring themed nightclubs and barn-sized pubs with live entertainment and boozy deals. In all Australian nightclubs, bars and casinos, entry is restricted to over-18s; the young and young-looking may have to show ID.

That said, there is a healthy and growing live music scene in Queensland, which cuts across various genres. Various venues support local, national and international acts – so keep your eye on billboards and the street press, and you may find yourself watching a band that's considered 'big' in their homeland in an intimate pub or club setting in Queensland.

For those with higher brows, Brisbane is your best bet for a bit of class. The **Queensland Performing Arts Centre** (www.qpac.com.au) in South Bank is the major hub for the city's cultural entertainment.

Nightlife venues and session times in Brisbane are listed in the daily *Courier-Mail*, and there are free publications such as *Rave, Time Off* and *Scene*, which can be picked up at venues and cafés. Try also www.brisbane247.com.

General listings for the Cairns area can be found in Friday's *Cairns Post*.

The following is just a very small selection of what else is on offer.

Brisbane

Albion Comedy Club and Restaurant

281 Sandgate Rd Albion; 3262 7308; www.brisbanecomedy.com.au
Slightly outside the city (few minutes in a taxi), the Albion puts on a range of professional comedy acts and open-mic nights, and twice a week they have live comedy hypnosis.

Alfred & Constance

Corner Alfred and Constance Streets, Fortitude Valley; tel: 3251 6500; www.alfredandconstance.com.au; Mon–Fri 7am–late, Sat–Sun 8am–late
With three bars and a cocktail list as long as Mr Tickle's arm, there's plenty to pour into yourself at A&C. Try a spiked Stonefruit Superstar for starters, or sip a long glass the Vanguard Beer Garden Bar. The White Lightening Tiki Bar is where the party will go on till late, but those who want to chill into the wee hours should park themselves in the Late Night Dessert Cafe and get a boozy smoothy from the Alcoholic Juice & Smoothy Station.

Brisbane Jazz Club

1 Annie Street, Kangaroo Point; tel: 3391 2006; www.brisbanejazzclub.com.au

Crowds at Brisbane Powerhouse Centre for the Arts

Right beside the river, near the Holman Street wharf, this characterful and intimate venue hosts occasional big-name acts, Brisbane's best traditional and contemporary jazz musicians and singers, and relaxed jam sessions. Check the website for the programme and session times.

Brisbane Powerhouse Centre for the Arts

119 Lamington Street, New Farm; tel: 3358 800; www.brisbanepowerhouse. com.au; box office Mon–Fri 9am–5pm, Sat noon–4pm

This world-class theatre, concert hall and experimental playhouse has an ever-changing repertoire and a focus on cutting-edge performances from Australia and overseas.

Cloudland

647 Ann Street, Fortitude Valley; tel: 3852 5000; www.cloudland.tv; Tue–Sun 11am–late

From outside, the spectacular geometric facade and rough wooden door give no indication that this is a nightspot, but inside a huge atrium shelters three levels of chic bars capped by a retractable roof. There are DJs, band residencies, dancing groups and all manner of live entertainment, along with reasonably priced drinks and a restaurant.

Family

8 McLachlan Street, Fortitude Valley; tel: 3852 5000; www.thefamily.com.au;

Fri–Sun 9pm–5am

Family has been voted Australia's best nightclub, with six bars, four levels, three music genres, massive sound and light technology, two huge dance floors and the capacity for 2,000 patrons. It attracts international DJs, musicians and a range of eclectic acts.

Mr & Mrs G

Eagle Street Pier 1 Eagle Street; tel: 3221 7001; www.mrandmrsg.com.au; daily noon–late

A cool new riverside cocktail bar has landed on the Eagle, one of Brisbane's premier eating streets. Named after the guv'nor and guv'noress, veteran restaurateurs, Andy and Marcia Georges, it has their signature stylish look. Get your ears tickled by live music here every Sunday.

Nant Whisky Cellar & Bar

Shop 10, Emporium, 1000 Ann Street, Fortitude Valley; tel: 3160 2633; www.nant. com.au; Tue–Thur 3pm–late, Fri–Sat noon–midnight

Nant is a single-malt whisky range from Tasmania, but in this emporium, which seats just 46 people, you can sample not only the namesake firewater, but also drams of more than 150 boutique whiskies from countries including Scotland, India, Wales, Ireland and Japan.

Newstead Brewing Co

85 Doggett Street, Newstead; tel: 3172

Hear Aboriginal stories while you dine at Flames of the Forest

2488; http://newsteadbrewing.com.au; daily 10am–midnight

Brisbane's oldest new craft brewery has a pub onsite, which stocks 12 draught beers, ales and ciders on tap - about two thirds of which are their own, the rest made of revolving selection of boutique beers from around the world. Food and take-away bottles of beer are available too.

Story Bridge Hotel

200 Main Street, Kangaroo Point; tel: 3391 2266; www.storybridgehotel.com.au; Mon–Thur 10am–midnight, Fri–Sat 10am–1.30am, Sun 8am–midnight

Situated under the famous bridge, this popular hotel has three bars and dining venues. Bands regularly play Thursday to Saturday nights, and there's live jazz on Sunday afternoons. Tales and Ales is a twice-weekly story telling and supping session where you can meet the head chef Jason Walker and learn about the beers and the brewery.

The Zoo

711 Ann Street; tel: 3854 1381; www.thezoo.com.au; Wed–Sat, times vary

Brisbane's granddaddy of live music venues champions indie acts on the whole, but also features reggae, jazz, hip hop and DJs if they're good enough. There's no dress code, and everybody is welcome, but they do have some eccentric (and endearing) house rules: no rum is sold (too much sugar makes people hyper) and no hardcore music acts are booked (stirs up the building's ghosts).

Gold Coast

Dracula's Cabaret Restaurant

1 Hooker Boulevard, Broadbeach Waters; tel: 5575 1000; www.draculas.com.au; daily 6pm–midnight

Part of Australia's longest-established theatre-restaurant chain, Dracula's features a dinner-cabaret show (currently 'Sin and Tonic') with magic, puppetry, musical productions and great comedy, all with classic horror themes, including a ghost train. Its blend of Burlesque, theatre and comedy isn't recommended for kids under 13.

The Arts Centre Gold Coast

135 Bundall Road, Surfers Paradise; tel: 5581 6500; www.theartscentregc.com.au

The Coast's nocturnal culture revolves around this centre. Live performances are a blend of Australian and international, old and new: Thursday is 'unplugged' in the Basement, Friday is usually comedy night, and Saturday night it's jazz. There's also a café, films, theatre and a gallery.

Airlie Beach

Down Under Bar

336 Shute Harbour Road, Airlie Beach; tel: 4948 2000; daily noon–2am

Surprisingly reasonable prices here, for both food and drinks, and it's a great venue for continuing the fun after the sun has left the party.

Gambling at the Reef Hotel Casino

Cairns

12 Bar Blue
62 Shields Street; tel: 4041 7388; Wed–Sun, 7pm–late

A refreshing change from beery backpacker joints, this intimate bar offers live jazz, blues and swing, jam sessions and open-mic nights for upcoming musicians.

Pier Bar & Grill
Pierpoint Road; tel: 4031 4677; www.pierbar.com.au; daily, 11.30am–late

Lively bar and restaurant, perfect for relaxing on the outdoor terrace to enjoy the sea views. Live music, DJs, dancing till late most nights, plus a highly popular Sunday afternoon session with music and cheap pizza

Reef Hotel Casino
35–41 Wharf Street; tel: 4030 8888; www.reefcasino.com.au; daily, times vary

The casino has more than 500 gaming machines and more than 40 tables, as well as restaurants, bars and various kinds of live entertainment, including the Velvet Underground nightclub.

Vibe Bar & Lounge
39-42 Lake Street; tel: 4052 1494; www.vibebarcairns.com; Mon–Thur 10.30–1am, Fri 10.30–5am, Sat noon–5am, Sun 5pm–3am

A centrally located restaurant that turns into a nightclub after hours, Vibe offers an appealing option to people who want neither the backpacker scene nor the casino culture, but who don't want to go to bed yet either. Each night has a different flavour, and the there's a sultry Sunday session to end the week.

The Woolshed
24 Shields Street, City Place; tel: 4031 6304; www.thewoolshed.com.au; daily 7pm–3am, Fri–Sat until 5am

Events and parties kick off every night of the week here, almost all of them involving the flashing of flesh to greater or lesser degrees. This is backpacker territory – open late and loud.

Port Douglas

Flames of the Forest
Tel: 4099 3144; www.flamesoftheforest. com.au; Tue, Thur–Sat 7.30–10pm

Dine in the rainforest and listen to Aboriginal stories: guests are picked up from their hotels from 6pm and transported to the Mowbray Valley, where candles flicker beside a stream. It's *Lord of the Rings* meets *Alice in Wonderland* to create an original and magical experience.

The Ironbar
5 Macrossan Street; tel: 4099 4776; www.ironbarportdouglas.com.au; daily 11am–late

A seven-nights a week venue that has been going forever, the Ironbar offers everything from cane toad racing to live music and karaoke. There's also a restaurant and it's open until 2am most nights for unsophisticated fun.

A–Z

A

Age restrictions

By law, to drink alcohol, smoke tobacco or get a tattoo in Queensland you must be 18 or over. Drivers in Queensland must be 17 years of age to obtain a provisional driving licence; visitors under 18 years of age will not be able to hire rental cars, and those under 25 will pay a premium.

Queensland is the only state in Australia to have a discrepancy in the legal minimum age assigned to different forms of sexual intercourse. The age of consent for vaginal sex is 16, but anal sex with anyone (male or female) under the age of 18 is punishable by law and can result in 14 years imprisonment.

B

Budgeting

Accommodation. A bed at a backpacker hostel can be as little as A\$25 a night, and a room in a three-star hotel is usually around A\$100. A room in a four- or five-star hotel can start as low as A\$200, although internet and low-season deals can halve even this tariff.

Airport taxi. A taxi from Brisbane Airport to central Brisbane will cost around A\$45. From Cairns Airport to central Cairns costs about A\$20. Train and/or bus options are also available.

Buses and ferries. A single (2-hour) ticket that allows travel on Brisbane's buses, trains and ferries within one zone costs around A\$5.20. If you're planning on being in the city for some time, consider getting a Go-Card, which will save you roughly 30 percent of what you'll pay if you continue using paper tickets.

Car rental. Renting a small car costs from A\$45 per day; a 4WD will cost A\$100-150 per day. Petrol (gasoline) costs around A\$1.20 per litre.

Dive courses. Prices range from A\$600–900 for courses that include open-water diving on day trips; more expensive courses include on-board accommodation and meals.

Restaurants. A main course in a budget restaurant costs about A\$15, A\$20–30 at a moderate restaurant, and A\$30–50 at an expensive restaurant. A bottle of Australian wine from a bottle shop (liquor store) starts at about A\$8; the same bottle in a restaurant is likely to cost A\$18, hence the popularity of BYO (Bring Your Own) restaurants. A glass of house wine averages around A\$8. A 'pot' of full-strength draught beer (see page 17) costs from A\$3.50, and a cup of espresso coffee or tea about the same.

Surf Rescue at Noosa

C

Children

Australia is a great place to travel with kids, and Queensland is particularly well suited to young families. Coastal Queensland is one big playground, from theme parks on the Gold Coast to koala cuddling at Australia Zoo and Cairns Tropical Zoo, to snorkelling on a coral reef. The Queensland Museum and Wheel of Brisbane on Brisbane's South Bank are sure to please, and at Tjapukai Aboriginal Cultural Park in Cairns the daily shows include an evening of corroboree around a fire. Child-concession admission usually applies to children 12 years and under, but it can be as old as 16. Check the *Yellow Pages* directory for professional baby-sitting services.

Clothing

In subtropical Brisbane, dress is informal and casual, though some hotels, restaurants and clubs will require a jacket and tie in the evening. Lightweight clothing is suitable year-round, but bring something warm in case the temperature drops at night, especially in autumn and winter. In Cairns's tropical climate, dress is always informal, with very few restaurants and clubs requiring a jacket and tie. Light-weight clothing is suitable all year round, but again bring something warm for cool winter nights in the highlands. To protect yourself against sunstroke and sunburn, you should wear sunscreen, a broad-brimmed hat, good sunglasses and a shirt with collar and sleeves. Bring swim-wear and rash vests (tightfitting, quick drying tops) for the beach.

Crime and safety

Brisbane, Cairns and the Gold Coast are fairly safe, but do not leave valuables unattended or in parked cars. Avoid dark, empty spaces and public toilets at night, and be aware of the potential of alcohol-fuelled violence around night-clubs. If visiting the Gold Coast, particularly the Sunshine Coast, avoid, if at all possible, the 'schoolies' season from the end of November to mid December, when huge numbers of teenagers descend on the place and basically get loaded. It's more annoying than dangerous – but it can certainly negatively affect your experience. The police are helpful and competent.

Customs

Non-dutiable allowances are 250g (8oz) of tobacco goods (approximately a carton of cigarettes) and 2,250ml (a quart) of beer, wine or spirits, and other dutiable goods to the total value of A$900, plus personal clothing, footwear and toiletries. Up to A$450-worth of dutiable goods, not including alcohol or tobacco, are allowed in the baggage of children under 18. Visit www.customs.gov.au for further information.

Strict quarantine regulations forbid the importation of foods, plants, animals and their by-products. Heavy jail

Looking out over Brisbane

penalties apply to the smuggling of drugs of any kind. Visitors are allowed to carry up to four weeks' supply of prescribed medications, but for larger supplies you should carry a doctor's certificate for customs purposes.

D

Disabled travellers

A useful booklet, *Accessible Queensland*, and information on other support services (available Mon–Fri) can be obtained from the Disability Information Awareness Line (DIAL), tel: 3224 8444 in Brisbane, or toll-free outside Brisbane on 1800 177 120 (international callers should dial +61 7 3224 8444).

E

Electricity

Electrical power is 240/250v AC, 50Hz Universal. Most hotels also have outlets for 110v (shavers only). Adaptors for Australian power outlets are readily available at the airport and in shops and hotels.

Embassies and consulates

The following are the closest contacts for travellers needing assistance when in Queensland.

British Consular Agency, Level 26 Waterfront Place, 1 Eagle Street, Brisbane; tel: 3223 3600; http://ukin australia.fco.gov.uk

Canadian Consulate General, Level 5, 111 Harrington Street, Sydney; tel: 02 9364 3000; recorded information: 02 9364 3050; www.international.gc.ca

Consulate General of Ireland, Level 26, 1 Market Street, Sydney; tel: 02 9264 9635; www.irishconsulatesydney.net

US Consulate General, MLC Centre, Level 10, 19–29 Martin Place, Sydney; tel: 02 9373 9200; after-hours emergencies, tel: 02 4422 2201; http://Sydney. usconsulate.gov

Emergencies

In an emergency, dial 000 for police, fire or ambulance services.

G

Gay and lesbian travellers

Queensland may not have quite the same gay sub-culture that you would find in Sydney, but there is a thriving gay community in the state's capital, and Noosa is a favoured spot to wind down after the Sydney Gay Mardi Gras in March.

To find the rainbow edge to Brisbane's nightlife, try The Wickham Hotel (www. thewickham.com.au) in Fortitude Valley or Spring Hill's Sportsman Hotel (www. sportsman hotel.com.au), the oldest gay bar in town. Brisbane's Pride Festival (www.brisbanepridefestival.com.au) is held each June. The highlight of the month-long festival is generally a parade and fair day.

Check out the gay press for further information; *Queensland Pride* is a free monthly newspaper, and *Q News* is a free fortnightly newspaper; both are based in

In Eumundi　　　　　　*Relaxing on the beach at Palm Cove*

Brisbane. Gay and Lesbian Tourism Australia (www.galta.com.au) promotes gay-friendly tourism operators.

Green issues

Queenslanders take environmental issues seriously, particularly in the heavily populated coastal regions. The recent decision by the Federal Australian Government to approve increased mining and industrial activity (including sea floor dredging and the dumping of silt) to take place in the World Heritage–listed Area of the Great Barrier Reef has caused a large amount of disquiet among local operators and environmentalists and the concerned public. For more information on this and other threats to the health of the Great Barrier Reef from mining activity, coral bleaching and other manmade issues, see www.greatbarrierreef.com.au For additional information on how climate change threatens the Great Barrier Reef, see www.gbrmpa.gov.au/corp_site/key_issues/climate_change. Recycling of glass, paper, aluminium and certain plastics is widespread; look for recycling bins with yellow lids.

Air travel produces a huge amount of carbon dioxide and is a significant contributor to global warming. If you would like to offset the damage caused to the environment by your flight, a number of organisations can do this for you, using online 'carbon calculators', which tell you how much you need to donate. In the UK travellers can visit www.climatecare.org or www.carbonneutral.com; in the US log on to www.climatefriendly.com or www.sustainabletravelinternational.org.

H

Health

Australia has excellent medical services. For medical attention out of working hours go to the casualty department of a major hospital or, if the matter is less urgent, visit one of the medical clinics in the major towns and tourist centres. Look under 'Medical Centres' or 'Medical Practitioners' in the *Yellow Pages*, or ask at your hotel.

Healthcare and insurance

Citizens of countries with which Australia has a reciprocal agreement (UK, Ireland, Finland, Norway, Sweden, Malta, Netherlands, New Zealand) are allowed restricted access to government Medicare service; this covers free care as a patient in hospital and subsidised medicines. It does not cover dental care, ambulance costs or emergency evacuation to your home country, so you are advised to take out your own travel insurance. Visitors from other countries should have private insurance to cover all medical care. See www.health.gov.au for details.

Inoculations

No vaccinations are necessary for entry into Australia unless you have visited an area (including parts of South America and Africa) infected by yellow fever, cholera or typhoid in the previous 14 days.

Natural health hazards

The biggest danger for travellers in Australia is the sun. Even on mild, cloudy days it has the potential to burn. Wear a broad-brimmed hat and, if you are planning on being out for a while, a long-sleeved shirt made from a light fabric. Wear SPF 30+ sunblock at all times, even under a hat.

Apart from jellyfish (see page 26), the main danger in north Queensland's coastal waters are saltwater (or estuarine) crocodiles. Do not enter waters where crocodile warning signs are posted, always ask for local advice, and if in doubt do not venture in. Some species of shark do pose a potential risk, albeit not as big as most people's fears lead them to believe. To be extra cautious, avoid swimming in murky water, with dogs or close to where pipes pump water or waste out to sea. Swimming in some areas – around the coast of Fraser Island for example – is actively discouraged. Listen to the advice of locals and always pay attention to warning signs on beaches. Scuba diving is very safe and takes place in extremely controlled conditions.

Pharmacies and hospitals

'Chemist shops' are a great place to go for advice on minor ailments such as bites, scratches and stomach trouble. They also stock a wide range of useful products such as sunblock, nappies (diapers) and non-prescription drugs. If you have a prescription from your doctor, and you want to take it to a pharmacist in Australia, you will need to have it endorsed by a local medical practitioner.

Hours and holidays

Business hours

Core business hours are Mon–Thur 9am–5.30pm, Fri until 9pm in the cities, Sat 9am–1pm. However, retailers tend to follow demand, and hours vary widely, with most shops in tourist precincts open on Saturday afternoon and Sunday.

Public holidays

Banks, post offices, government and private offices close on the following holidays:

New Year's Day (1 Jan)
Australia Day (26 Jan)
Good Friday (date variable)
Easter Monday (date variable)
Anzac Day (25 April)
Labour Day (First Monday in May)
Queen's Birthday (2nd Monday in June)
Christmas Day (25 Dec)
Boxing Day (26 Dec)

Internet facilities

Internet cafés have proliferated in recent years, and travellers to Australia should have no trouble finding internet access in major cities and tourist locations.

Always heed danger signs at the beach

Many standard cafés, pubs and restaurants offer free Wi-fi (be sure to buy something at least once an hour). Most hotels and hostels now have facilities for people travelling with their own laptops – although some persist in charging per minute or hour – and local libraries fill the gap in communities where there is no commercial internet facility.

L

Left luggage

At Brisbane Airport there are left-luggage facilities in the international terminal but not in the domestic terminal. Cairns Airport has a baggage-storage facility run by Smart Carte Australia (tel: 0407 359 678). There are lockers for luggage on all levels of Brisbane's Transit Centre at Roma Street. To check the facilities available at other Queensland train stations, see www.queenslandrail-travel.com.au.

Lost property

Report loss or theft of valuables to the police immediately, as most insurance policies insist on a police report. In Brisbane, lost property found at a Citytrain station is held for three days at that particular station before being forwarded to Roma Street Station (tel: 3235 1859 Mon–Fri 10.15am–2.25pm.For anything left on Brisbane's ferries, tel: 3229 7778, daily 9am–5.30pm.

To locate property left on a Brisbane bus, contact the Brisbane City Council call centre, tel: 3403 8888. The lost-property office is located at 69 Ann Street, Brisbane.

M

Maps

Officially accredited Visitor Information Centres, indicated by the yellow 'i' against a blue background, give away useful maps of their areas. The Queensland Holidays website carries a map of Queensland showing the locations of the Visitor Centres. Visit the RACQ Travel Centres (www.racq.com.au) for touring maps. They can also be mailed overseas to international visitors.

Media

Print and online media

Brisbane's daily newspaper is the *Courier-Mail* (www.couriermail.com.au), a lively tabloid published Monday to Saturday. On Sunday the major Brisbane newspaper is the *Sunday Mail*. Both are part of the News Corporation stable. In Cairns the local daily is the *Cairns Post* (www.cairns.com.au).

Australia has two national papers, the *Australian* (www.theaustralian.com.au) and the *Australian Financial Review* (www.afr.com). In 2013, the British paper *The Guardian* launched an Australian version of the paper online: www.theguardian.com/au. Foreign-language newspapers and magazines are available at newsagents in Brisbane, the airport and major tourist districts.

Cairns marina

Radio and television

The Australian Broadcasting Commission (ABC) runs national television channels as well as an extensive network of radio stations. ABC television offers excellent news and current affairs, as well as local and imported drama, comedy, sports and cultural programmes. The commercial TV stations, Channels 7, 9 and 10, offer news, drama, soaps, infotainment, travel shows and, between them, coverage of most of the major international sporting events. Foxtel (www.foxtel.com.au) is the major pay television company in the country, operating cable, direct broadcast satellite television and IPTV services. Many hotels provide access to a large number of cable television stations.

Radio stations include Triple J (107.7 FM in Brisbane and 107.5 in Cairns, or listen online from anywhere www.abc.net.au/triplej), rock and comment for the twentysomethings; Classic FM (106.1 FM in Brisbane and 105.9 FM, www.abc.net.au/classic), continuous classical music; and Radio National (792 AM and 105.1 FM in Cairns, www.abc.net.au/radionational), excellent national news and events coverage. Commercial radio stations include Triple M FM (104.7 in Brisbane, www.triplem.com.au/brisbane) for popular local and international rock, and Nova 1069 for contemporary music (106.9 FM, www.novafm.com.au/station/nova1069).

Of particular interest to overseas travellers is Australia's ethnic/multicultural broadcaster, SBS (www.sbs.com.au). The organisation's excellent television channel offers many foreign-language films and documentaries, and Australia's best coverage of world news. SBS Radio (93.3 FM in Brisbane, www.sbs.com.au/radio) offers programmes in a variety of languages.

Money

The four major banks in Australia are ANZ, Commonwealth, National Australia and Westpac. There's also the Bank of Queensland (www.boq.com.au). Trading hours are generally Mon–Thur 9am–4pm and Fri 9am–5pm.

Cash machines

Most bank branches have automatic teller machines (ATMs) that are networked with Cirrus, Maestro and other networks, allowing you to access funds from overseas accounts. Many will charge you to withdraw cash.

Credit cards

Most establishments display a list of the credit cards they will accept, usually including MasterCard and Visa, and less so Amex, Diners Club and JCB.

Currency

Australia's currency is the dollar (A$), which is divided into 100 cents. Notes come in denominations of 5, 10, 20, 50 and 100 dollars, each of which has a distinctly different colour. Coins come in denominations of 5, 10, 20 and 50

The old Cairns Post building

cents (silver-coloured), and one and two dollars (bronze-coloured). The one-dollar coin is, confusingly, larger than the two. There are no one- or two-cent coins, so shopkeepers round up change to the nearest five cents.

Taxes

The Australian government collects a 10 percent goods and services tax (GST) on virtually all retail sales. Under a 'tourist refund scheme', the GST on goods valued at over A$300, bought from the same shop within the previous 30 days and carried as hand luggage, can be recovered upon leaving the country at a Tourist Refund Scheme (TRS) booth located beyond customs at the airport; you must have retained the tax invoice. For more details, go here: http://www.customs.gov.au/site/page4646.asp.

Tipping

Tipping is not customary even for taxi drivers and restaurant staff, but it is not unusual to reward good service with a gratuity of between 10 and 15 percent of the bill. Hotel staff do not solicit or expect tips, but certainly will not be offended by one.

Travellers' cheques

It is becoming increasingly uncommon for people to use travellers' cheques, but all well-known brands can be exchanged at banks, five-star hotels and exchange bureaus.

P

Police

In an emergency call 000. At other times call the local police station, which can be located on www.police.qld.gov.au

Post

Australian Post (http://auspost.com.au) offices are open Mon–Fri 9am–5pm; some post shops are also open Sat 9am–noon. The Brisbane GPO (261 Queen Street) is open Mon–Fri 7am–6pm. The main post office in Cairns is at 13 Grafton Street (Mon–Fri 8.30am–5.30pm). Post offices will hold properly addressed mail for visitors and sell stamps, standard and Express Post envelopes and packaging. Post boxes are red (standard mail) or yellow (Express Post).

The cost of overseas mail depends on the weight and size of the package. To send a postcard to Europe or the USA costs A$2.60. A letter up to 50g in weight will also cost A$2.60.

S

Smoking

In Queensland it is illegal to smoke inside restaurants, bars and clubs, including commercial outdoor eating or drinking areas, at patrolled beaches and major sports stadiums. Additionally, it is illegal to smoke in a car carrying children under the age of 16.

T

Telephones

The international code for Australia is 61 and the area code for Queensland is 07. Within Queensland, you do not need to dial this code.

To call from Australia, dial 0011 + country code + area code (drop the first 0) + number. The country code for Canada and the US is 1, Ireland is 353 and the UK is 44.

There are plenty of public telephones and most take phone cards. All Australian coins can be used in payphones, though many public phones only use phone cards, which can be bought in general stores, post offices and newsagents. For eight-figure numbers, you dial the 07 area code only if you're calling from outside Queensland. For Directory Assistance, dial 1223.

Mobile (cell) phones

The GSM 900 mobile phone system network in Australia is compatible with systems everywhere except Japan and the Americas. To use your mobile here for a short term you should buy an Australian SIM card with prepaid calls. Providers include Telstra (www.telstra.com), Optus (www.optus.com.au), Vodaphone (www.vodafone.com.au) and Virgin Mobile (www.virginmobile.com.au).

Time zones

Queensland operates on Australian Eastern Standard Time (Greenwich Mean Time plus 10 hours). Daylight saving is not observed in Queensland, but does apply, from different dates, in the other states across three time zones, giving, at worst, up to six differing times across the country.

Tourist information

Before you leave home, see the Tourism Australia website, www.australia.com. Queensland is well served by organisations designed to help visitors. In addition to information centres, the following websites will answer almost any questions that you might have: www.experiencequeensland.com; www.queenslandholidays.com.au

The main tourist information centres in Queensland are:

Brisbane
Corner Albert and Queen streets; tel: 3006 6290; www.ourbrisbane.com, and the Southern Queensland Visitors Information Centre, Level 2, Brisbane International Airport; tel: 3406 3190; www.southernqueensland.com.au

Cairns
Tourism Tropical North Queensland; 51 The Esplanade; tel: 4051 3588; www.tropicalaustralia.com.au

Gold Coast
Cavill Avenue, Surfers Paradise; tel: 1300 309 440; www.visitgoldcoast.com

Mission Beach
Porters Promenade; tel: 4068 7099; www.missionbeachtourism.com

Qantas is a major Australian airline

Noosa

Hastings Street, Noosa Heads; tel: 5447 4988; www.tourismnoosa.com.au

Whitsunday Coast

Tourism Whitsundays; Bruce Highway, Proserpine; tel: 4945 3711; www.whitsundaytourism.com

Transport

Airports

Many international airlines provide regular links between Brisbane Airport (www.bne.com.au) and Europe, the US and Asian and Pacific nations. Frequent Qantas and Virgin Blue domestic services fly to Brisbane and Coolangatta (www.goldcoastairport.com.au) from Sydney, Melbourne, Canberra and cities.

Brisbane Airport's adjacent international and domestic terminals are connected by shuttle bus. Few hotels provide regular courtesy coach transfers, but some will do so on request. Cabs to the city are expensive. However, a combination of comfortable, regular Airport Commuter coaches and a fast shuttle train takes you to and from the central city terminal at Roma Street with shuttles from there to many of the downtown hotels. Translink (tel: 131230; www.translink.com.au) can provide all the travel information you need. A cab ride to the central business district costs about A$45.

Cairns Airport (www.cairnsair port.com) has regular air links to Asia and the Pacific as well as to Brisbane, Sydney and Melbourne. The airport is 8km (5 miles) from central Cairns. Many hotels provide coach transfers, or Sun Palm's Express Coaches (tel: 4087 2900; www.sunpalmtransport.com) cost A$10 to Cairns hotels. Airport Connection (tel: 4098 2800; www.tnqshuttle.com) services Port Douglas, Mission Beach and Cape Tribulation.

Public transport

Translink (tel: 131230; www.translink.com.au) is responsible for the state's bus, train and ferry transport.

Rail and long-distance bus

Brisbane's main rail terminal is the Transit Centre in Roma Street, a short taxi ride to/from most Brisbane hotels. Fast trains travel to Robina on the Gold Coast, from 4am to 11pm, at half-hour intervals most of the day, every hour during less busy times. The *Sunlander* rail service (three times weekly) along the coast from Brisbane to Cairns takes about 31.5 hours. The faster *Tilt Train* (twice weekly) takes just over 24 hours. Contact Queensland Rail's Traveltrain Holidays (tel: 1300 132 722; www.queenslandrailtravel.com.au).

Coaches to Surfers Paradise, Southport and other Coast destinations are provided by Surfside Buslines (www.surfside.com.au). Both Greyhound Australia (www.greyhound.com.au) and Premier Motor Service (www.premierms.com.au) service all the major resort towns along the East Coast between Brisbane and Cairns; the direct journey between the two cities takes 29 hours.

Brisbane's ANZAC square

Taxis

Taxis showing a light can be flagged down from the kerb. Rates per km are around A$1, plus an A$4 initial charge. A small phone booking fee is charged if you call a cab, and most cabs take credit cards. Taxis normally carry only four passengers, but maxi-cabs, which take six to 10 passengers, are available on request at 1.5 times normal rates. Passengers may not smoke in cabs and can be fined if not wearing a seatbelt. To book a cab (just about anywhere in Australia) call tel: 131 008.

Car rental

International car-hire companies offer good discounts on pre-booked hires, with the option to return the vehicle to another major centre at no extra charge. The minimum age for hiring a car is 18, but drivers under 25 pay a surcharge. A national driving licence is acceptable if it is written in English; otherwise you should obtain an international driver's licence.

Insurance on conventional rental cars is invalid on unsealed (dirt) roads, but most hire companies will insure 4WD vehicles for any road. Cover for single-vehicle accidents is subject to a high excess payment. Major international rental firms include:

Avis (tel: 13 63 33; www.avis.com.au) **Budget** (tel: 1300 362 848; www.budget.com.au)

Europcar (tel: 1300 131 390; www.europcar.com.au)

Hertz (tel: 13 30 39; www.hertz.com.au)

Thrifty (tel: 1300 367 227; www.thrifty.com.au).

Driving

Traffic drives on the left in Australia, so you usually give way to the right and road signs usually match international rules. There is a 0.05 percent blood alcohol limit for drivers, which is widely enforced by the practice of random breath tests. Police also conduct random drug tests – both involve stopping entire lanes of traffic, or even whole roads.

Off-road driving

When driving on sand it is always advisable to carry a 'snatch strap' in the event of getting bogged in loose sand. Check with your 4WD hire company that you have one in your vehicle. Also consult them for the correct tyre pressure for your vehicle. Queensland boasts the full podium when it comes to big sand islands: Fraser Island, the world's biggest, North Stradbroke, the second biggest, and Moreton Island, which takes bronze. To drive on any of these islands you must get a Vehicle Access Permit from the Department of Parks, Recreation, Sport and Racing (NPRSR), go here for more information: http://nprsr.qld.gov.au/recreation-areas/vehicle_access_permit_fees.html. Lowering pressure in your tyres makes driving on sand safer and easier. However, do not forget to re-inflate your tyres once again when driving on bitumen. Also note that speed limits are signposted and enforced.

A Brisbane taxi rank   *Cycling over Goodwill Bridge in Brisbane*

Tours

If you don't fancy driving your own 4WD, take a guided day tour. Many operators offer these from Brisbane including Goanna Adventures (tel: 3841 7781; www.goannaadventures.com.au) and Sunrover Expeditions (tel: 1800 353 717; www.sunrover.com.au). Alternatively, take the Tangalooma Launch and book a Tangalooma Resort tour (tel: 3637 2000; www.tangalooma.com).

You can also take a guided tour of Fraser Island from Brisbane and Hervey Bay; operators include Cool Dingo Tours (www.cooldingotour.com), Sunrover Expeditions (www.sunrover.com.au) and Bushwacker Ecotours (www.bushwacker-ecotours.com.au). Another option is to join one of the resort's ranger-guided day tours from Kingfisher Bay Resort.

V

Visas and passports

Your passport must be valid for at least six months from your date of arrival into Australia. All non-Australian citizens need a valid visa to enter Australia, with the exception of New Zealand citizens travelling on New Zealand passports, who are issued with a visa on arrival in Australia. Visas are available from Australian visa offices such as Australian embassies, high commissions and consulates, and from travel agents and airlines in some countries.

The **Electronic Transfer Authority** (ETA) enables visitors to obtain a visa on the spot from their travel agent or airline office. The system is in place in over 30 countries, including the UK and the US. ETA visas are generally valid over a 12-month period; single stays must not exceed three months, but return visits within the 12-month period are allowed. ETAs are issued free, or you can purchase one online for A\$20 from www.eta.immi. gov.au.

Most EU citizens are eligible for an **eVisitor** visa, which is free and can be obtained online. **Tourist visas** are available for continuous stays longer than three months, but must be obtained from an Australian visa office, such as an embassy or consulate. A A\$20 fee applies. Those travelling on any kind of tourist visa are not permitted to work while in Australia.

Working Holiday Visas are obtainable for citizens of some countries (including the United Kingdom, Canada, France, Germany, the Netherlands and Ireland) who are between the ages of 18 and 31.

The concept behind the visa is to encourage cultural exchange and closer ties between Australia and eligible countries. People must be outside Australia when they apply for their first Working Holiday visa and when the visa is decided. The initial period of the visa is 12 months, but in certain circumstance (such as if the visa holder spends a period working in a rural area where there is a labour shortage) it can be extended for a further year. For more information, visit www.immi. gov.au/Visas/Pages/417.aspx

Steve Irwin, the Crocodile Hunter

BOOKS AND FILM

Queensland may not enjoy a rich literary or cinematic tradition, but the immense landscapes, dramatic conditions and eccentric population of the East Coast has produced a few great actors – among them Australia's most venerated, Geoffrey Rush, and indigenous star Deborah Mailman – and inspired some notable writers and filmmakers.

Film

One of Australia's most popular screen characters ever was based on a true-blue Queensland icon: *Amphiprion ocellaris*, otherwise known as the anemonefish or the clown fish. **Finding Nemo** (2003) was a colossal global hit, somewhat ironically causing a massive spike in number of clown fish being kept in captivity around the world.

Steve Irwin's **The Crocodile Hunter: Collision Course** (2002) may have proved that acting wasn't the great man's strongest suit, but the film – about a crocodile that swallows a piece of space junk that turns out to be a transmitting beacon which could change the axis of global power – was an unlikely international success.

It's worth mentioning that Paul Hogan's beloved **Crocodile Dundee** (1986) did all his best work in Queensland's tropics, before hopping off to New York to demonstrate what a real knife looks like. The pub that appears in the film is the Walkabout Creek Hotel in McKinlay, a one-camel town in the remote northwest of the state.

Queensland's more critically acclaimed big screen appearances include a starring role in **The Proposition** (2005), a brutally gritty Australian western written by the dark pen of Nick Cave and featuring the acting talents of British heavyweights Ray Winstone, John Hurt and Emily Watson, along with local luminaries Guy Pearce, Noah Taylor, David Wenham and indigenous actor David Gulpilil. Set in the 1880s, the film was shot on location in the blistering heat of Winton, deep in the Queensland outback, hundreds of kilometres east of Mackay.

This harsh terrain inspired Queenslander George Miller, writer and director of the cultish **Mad Max** films (1979–1981), to create his dystopian world and the antihero that launched the career of Mel Gibson (who famously scored the role after auditioning with a battered face, having been in a drunken brawl the night before).

Miller, from Chinchilla in the Darling Ranges of the Gold Coast's hinterland, later wrote the **Happy Feet** (2006), a kids' film with an environmental sub-message about a group of singing-and-dancing penguins, which starred the voices of numerous Australians including Hugh Jackman and Steve Irwin (who died during production).

Clown fish   *Peter Carey*

Other notable films wholly or partially shot in Queensland include the rom-com **Muriel's Wedding** (1994) starring Australians Toni Collette and Rachel Griffiths, which features scenes shot in Coolangatta, the Gold Coast, Surfers Paradise and Hamilton Island – and the crime comedy **Gettin' Square** (2004), with Sam Worthington, David Wenham, Gary Sweet and British actor Timothy Spall.

And then there's the shark-based horror genre, to which Queensland has contributed two films – **Open Water** (2003) and **The Reef** (2010) – both loosely based on true stories, the latter a shipwreck yarn and the first a tale about an American couple who get left behind by their boat while on a scuba-diving trip to the Great Barrier Reef (which did actually happen to Tom and Eileen Lonergan in 1998 – but thankfully, the rules are much tighter today).

Arguably the greatest work completed with cameras in Queensland, though, was the three-part series **The Great Barrier Reef** (screened in 2012), filmed by the BBC's peerless nature-documentary makers and narrated by marine biologist Monty Halls.

Books

Brisbane-based writer Nick Earls has been likened to British pop-culture scribe Nick Hornby. Earls writes poignant and funny novels about everyday life. His award-winning books include **Zigzag Street** and the young-adult novel, **48 Shades of Brown**.

British-born but Queensland raised, John Birmingham initially found fame with **He Died With A Felafel In His Hand** and **The Tasmanian Babes Fiasco**. The first is a tragicomic account of life in shared accommodation around Australia, based on Birmingham's own experiences, which was later turned into a film. *The Tasmanian Babes Fiasco* was re-interpreted by 36 unemployed actors, who turned it into Australian's longest-running stage play.

Birmingham has since explored different genres, with techno thriller **Weapons of Choice**, his **Axis of Time** trilogy and a series – **Without Warning**, **After America** and **Angels of Vengeance** – an imaginative look at the world after American society has been destroyed by an apocalyptic energy field.

One of Australia's most highly regarded authors is Peter Carey – a two-time winner of the Booker prize (for *Oscar and Lucinda* and *True History of the Kelly Gang*). While Queensland can't claim Carey, he did write his first published novel *Bliss* (1981) while living in an alternative community called Starlight in Yandina, north of Brisbane – an experience that clearly influences the narrative.

Brisbane-born David Malouf, whose epic *The Great World* (1990) – which recounts the experiences of two Australians through the World Wars – won him the Commonwealth Writers' Prize and the French Prix Femina Étranger, was also shortlisted for the Booker Prize for his novel *Remembering Babylon*.

ABOUT THIS BOOK

This *Explore Guide* has been produced by the editors of Insight Guides, whose books have set the standard for visual travel guides since 1970. With top-quality photography and authoritative recommendations, these guidebooks bring you the very best routes and itineraries in the world's most exciting destinations.

BEST ROUTES

The routes in the book provide something to suit all budgets, tastes and trip lengths. As well as covering the destination's many classic attractions, the itineraries track lesser-known sights. The routes embrace a range of interests, so whether you are an art fan, a gourmet, a history buff or have kids to entertain, you will find an option to suit.

We recommend reading the whole of a route before setting out. This should help you to familiarise yourself with it and enable you to plan where to stop for refreshments – options are shown in the 'Food and Drink' box at the end of each tour.

For our pick of the tours by theme, consult Recommended Routes for... (see pages 4–5).

INTRODUCTION

The routes are set in context by this introductory section, giving an overview of the destination to set the scene, plus background information on food and drink, shopping and more, while a succinct history timeline highlights the key events over the centuries.

DIRECTORY

Also supporting the routes is a Directory chapter, with a clearly organised A–Z of practical information, our pick of where to stay while you are there and select restaurant listings; these eateries complement the more low-key cafés and restaurants that feature within the routes and are intended to offer a wider choice for evening dining. Also included here are some nightlife listings and our recommendations for books and films about the destination.

ABOUT THE AUTHORS

Patrick Kinsella, a freelance journalist and editor, has the good fortune to be a dual citizen of Australia and the UK, enabling him to enjoy the delights of both and experience their vastly contrasting wonders with new eyes each time he swaps hemispheres. He spent much of the last decade mountain biking across the Tablelands behind Cairns and Port Douglas, hiking across the Hinterland behind the Gold Coast, diving extensively along the Great Barrier Reef, sipping cold beers on beaches throughout the state and enjoying great coffee in the increasingly bohemian backstreets of Brisbane.

This book builds on original content by Lindsay Brown, a former marine biologist who now divides his time between Australia and South Asia writing travel guides, and Cathy Finch, a Queensland-based writer and photographer.

CONTACT THE EDITORS

We hope you find this Explore Guide useful, interesting and a pleasure to read. If you have any questions or feedback on the text, pictures or maps, please do let us know. If you have noticed any errors or outdated facts, or have suggestions for places to include on the routes, we would be delighted to hear from you. Please drop us an email at insight@apaguide.co.uk. Thanks!

CREDITS

Explore Queensland
Contributors: Patrick Kinsella & Lindsay Brown
Commissioning Editor: Sarah Clark
Series Editor: Sarah Clark
Pictures/Art: Tom Smyth/Shahid Mahmood
Map Production: original cartography
Phoenix Mapping, updated by Apa
Cartography Department
Production: Tynan Dean & Rebeka Davies
Photo credits: Alamy 17R, 20, 40/41, 52/53;
Aria 4/5T, 110/111, 113; AWL Images 84;
Brisbane Powerhouse 121; Cairns Regional
Gallery 4BC, 73R; Cairns Tropical Zoo 82;
Cairns Wildlife Dome 75R; CITY publicity 116;
Coffee Works Experience 90; Coral Princess
Cruises 26, 28/29, 32ML; Coral Sea Resort
109; Dreamstime 41R, 54/55, 70, 123,
132/133, 136/137; E'cco Bistro 112; Flames
of the Forest 122; Fotolia 95; Getty Images
6/7, 68/69; iStockphoto 4TL, 5MR, 15,
50/51, 64, 94, 98MC, 104, 114, 115R, 117;
Jerry Dennis/Apa Publications 16/17; John
Gollings 2ML; Jungle Surfing 87; Kingfisher
Bay Resort 63, 64/65; Kuranda Scenic
Railway 78, 78/79; Kuranda Skyrail 76; Mark
Pokorny/Queensland Folk Federation Inc 21;
Mary Evans Picture Library 30; Moviestore
Collection/Rex 136; O'Reilly's Guesthouse
60, 61R; Ochre Restaurant 118; Oskars
Restaurant 32MR, 119; Palazzo Versace 108;
Peter Stuckings/Apa Publications 1, 2MC,
2MR, 2MR, 2/3T, 5MR, 6ML, 6MC, 6MR, 8, 9,
10, 11R, 10/11, 13R, 12/13, 16, 18, 19, 22,
32MC, 32MR, 32ML, 32MC, 32/33T, 34, 35R,
34/35, 36, 37R, 36/37, 38, 39R, 38/39,
40, 42, 43, 48, 49, 50, 51R, 56, 56/57, 57R,
58, 58/59, 59R, 60/61, 62, 71, 72, 72/73,
74, 74/75, 77, 82/83, 83R, 86, 88, 89, 91R,
90/91, 92/93, 98ML, 98MR, 98ML, 98/99T,
102, 102/103, 106/107, 114/115, 120,
124/125, 126, 126/127, 127R, 128/129,
130, 131, 134, 134/135, 135R; Pictures
Colour Library 85; PA Images 137R; Quicksilver and Great Adventures 28, 29R; Raging
Thunder 23R; Spirit of Freedom 26/27, 27R;
Stamford Hotels and Resorts 100, 101; State
Library of Queensland 31; Tangalooma Island
Resort 4MC, 44/45, 46, 105; Tanks Art Centre
4/5M; Tjapukai Aboriginal Cultural Park 6MR,
12; Tourism Port Douglas & Daintree 22/23,
80/81, 98MR; Tourism Queensland 2MC,
6ML, 14, 46/47, 47R, 54, 55R, 65R, 66,
67, 96, 97; Treasury Casino and Hotel 103R;
Village in the Rainforest 79R; Warner Village

Theme Parks 2ML, 4ML, 6MC, 24, 25, 98MC
Cover credits: Front Cover Main: Cairns,
Palm Cove jetty at dawn with Haycock
Island, *Corbis*; Front Cover BL: Story Bridge,
Brisbane, *Peter Stuckings/Apa Publications*;
Back Cover: (Left) Prawn trawlers on the
Australian coast of North Stradbroke Island,
Dreamstime; (Right): Clown fish on australias
great barrier reef, *Dreamstime*

Printed by CTPS – China
© 2014 Apa Publications (UK) Ltd
All Rights Reserved
First Edition 2014

No part of this book may be reproduced,
stored in a retrieval system or transmitted
in any form or by any means (electronic,
mechanical, photocopying, recording or
otherwise), without prior written permission
of APA Publications. Brief text quotations with
use of photographs are exempted for book
review purposes only. Information has been
obtained from sources believed to be reliable,
but its accuracy and completeness, and the
opinions based thereon, are not guaranteed.
  Although Insight Guides and the authors
of this book have taken all reasonable care in
preparing it, we make no warranty about the
accuracy or completeness of its content, and,
to the maximum extent permitted, disclaim all
liability arising from its use.

DISTRIBUTION

Worldwide
APA Publications GmbH & Co. Verlag KG
(Singapore branch)
7030 Ang Mo Kio Ave 5, 08-65
Northstar @ AMK, Singapore 569880
Email: apasin@singnet.com.sg
UK and Ireland
Dorling Kindersley Ltd (a Penguin Company)
80 Strand, London, WC2R 0RL, UK
Email: sales@uk.dk.com
US
Ingram Publisher Services
One Ingram Blvd, PO Box 3006, La Vergne,
TN 37086-1986
Email: ips@ingramcontent.com
Australia and New Zealand
Woodslane, 10 Apollo St, Warriewood NSW
2102, Australia
Email: info@woodslane.com.au

INDEX

MAP LEGEND

● Start of tour

⟶ Tour & route direction

❶ Recommended sight

❷ Recommended
	restaurant/café

★ Place of interest

❶ Tourist information

𝟏 Statue/monument

✉ Main post office

🚌 Main bus station

⤌ Viewpoint

Park

Important building

Hotel

Transport hub

Market/store

Pedestrian area

Urban area

INSIGHT GUIDES

INSPIRING YOUR NEXT ADVENTURE

Insight Guides offers you a range of travel guides
to match your needs. Whether you are looking for
inspiration for planning a trip, cultural information,
walks and tours, great listings, or practical advice, we
have a product to suit you.

www.insightguides.com